D0499963

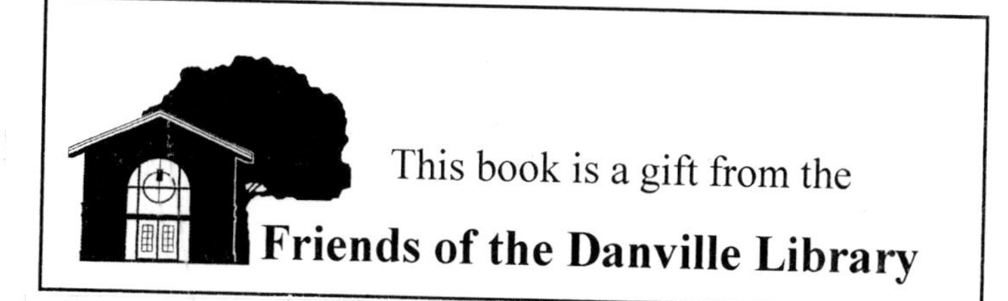
This book is a gift from the
Friends of the Danville Library

THE AGE CURVE

The Age Curve

How to Profit from the Coming Demographic Storm

KENNETH W. GRONBACH

AMACOM AMERICAN MANAGEMENT ASSOCIATION
New York • Atlanta • Brussels • Chicago • Mexico City • San Francisco
Shang[illegible] ashington, D.C.

Special discounts on bulk quantities of AMACOM books are available to corporations, professional associations, and other organizations. For details, contact Special Sales Department, AMACOM, a division of American Management Association, 1601 Broadway, New York, NY 10019.
Tel: 212-903-8316. Fax: 212-903-8083. E-mail: specialsls@amanet.org
Website: www.amacombooks.org/go/specialsales
To view all AMACOM titles go to: www.amacombooks.org

Library of Congress Cataloging-in-Publication Data

Gronbach, Kenneth W.
The age curve : how to profit from the coming demographic storm / Kenneth W. Gronbach.
p. cm.
Includes index.
ISBN-13: 978-0-8144-0181-1
ISBN-10: 0-8144-0181-3
1. Target marketing—United States. 2. Consumer behavior—United States. 3. Marketing research—United States. 4. Demography—United States. I. American Management Association. II. Title.

HF5415.127.G76 2008
658.8'343—dc22

2008014101

Printed in the United States of America.

Printing number
10 9 8 7 6 5 4 3 2 1

FOR LINDA . . .

CONTENTS

FOREWORD

You are about to read a book that could change your perspective forever. Books like this are rare and should be savored. Ken Gronbach's book is so compelling, and his writing is so direct, that you'll probably read it in a day or two.

When we hear a good idea we say, "That's so simple and so obvious. Why didn't I think of it?" Ken's good idea—a brilliant recognition, really—is that the size of successive U.S. generations, and thus the differing number of people in specific age groups, is at the heart of the long-term sea changes we experience in economics, business, and society.

By good fortune I invited Ken to speak at the university in Connecticut where I was director of the entrepreneurship program. My entrepreneurship and marketing students organized and promoted the event, and his idea—the simple yet profound truth you'll read in the following pages—captivated the audience of businesspeople, faculty, and students.

The most remarkable part of that lecture—and a feature I shall always remember—was the way Ken used visuals. In stark contrast to virtually every lecture I have ever attended or given, Ken spent the entire ninety minutes with only *one slide* projected on the screen. That slide, which summarized and proved each of his points, and which is the basis of this book, is a count of the number of live births in each year from 1905 to 2006. Simple? Yes. Profound? More than you can imagine.

Entrepreneurship starts with recognizing opportunities and developing products and services that capitalize on an opportunity for a specific market. What the volumes of research on opportunity recognition and market definition leave out is Ken's basic insight: Neither an amazing product, nor a perfect business plan, nor an unlimited marketing budget will compensate for the fundamental ebbs and flows of population. Markets are always growing or decreasing, not because of changes in preference, but because the literal number of people within any given cohort is vastly different than even five years before.

In short, Ken argues that most of the demand-side elements of a market cannot be influenced. They are due to demographic size and changes in the target markets themselves, from the tiny and rapidly diminishing Silent Generation (whose members are now in their sixties and seventies), to the enormous Baby Boom Generation, to the surprisingly small number of Gen Xers now in their twenties and thirties, to the much more massive Generation Y, the majority of which is still in middle school and high school.

Even more startling are the social implications of Ken's insight. Politicians take credit for crime reduction, but are crime percentages actually lower, or are there fewer people (in the average crime-committing ages of fifteen to thirty) who commit the crimes? Is the decreasing abortion rate a reflection of conservative values or does it simply reflect a decrease in the number of women likely to have an abortion? When diversity increases in U.S. business, is it a "win" for liberal policymakers or is it due to the deaths of long-standing corporate board members whose business success (and bigoted values) were hewn well before the Civil Rights era?

Ken derives similar implications for future unemployment rates, education levels, economic growth rates, and more. He explains why hugely successful companies like Levi Strauss have had precipitous drops in revenues and why previously successful companies like Ames are now out of business. And he can direct you to your next multimillion-dollar market, as well as explain why your previous product was a failure.

Without a doubt his explanations leave out crucial factors, and his unorthodox approach may at first appear flip and even a bit imprudent. But if you focus on the spirit of his argument, you will expand your perceptions and dramatically improve your strategic business planning. Ever since listening to Ken's lecture a few years ago, I have added new topic areas into my business school courses, altered some of my consulting approaches, and learned how to look at business opportunities in a much more focused way. I hope and trust that this book will serve as a beacon to you as well, expanding your understanding, enhancing your perspectives, and increasing your creative, effective action in business, policy making, and life. Enjoy!

Benyamin B. Lichtenstein
Professor of Entrepreneurship and Management
University of Massachusetts, Boston

INTRODUCTION

There are sick empty feelings in your stomach, and then there are really big sick empty feelings. I had the latter. Our signature account of eight years, American Honda Motorcycle, had shipped the year's allotment of new 1986 bikes to the dealers two months earlier and a unique thing happened: nothing.

Our history with Honda had been nothing but successful up to this point. The formula was simple: Honda sent the bikes from Japan to a New Jersey warehouse, where they were distributed to the Northeast regional dealers, who prepped them and displayed them on showroom floors. As soon as they were displayed at the dealerships, the marketing and advertising kicked in and the customers bought them—all of them. Life was good.

But this was 1986 and the bikes did not sell. It wasn't that traffic was slow. There was *no* traffic. The folks at Honda asked, "Did you run the ads?"

This is when the really big sick empty feeling kicked in. The bad news was that sales volume was dropping like a stone. The really bad news was that sales would continue to drop for the next six years until the decline amounted to an 80 percent free fall. Gulp. By 1992 most of the dealerships were ready to close, and we lost the account. No surprise there. The only consolation was that exactly the same thing happened to Yamaha, Suzuki, and Kawasaki. Someone had turned off the faucet and we didn't know who or why.

In mid-October 1996 I was reading the *Hartford Courant's* editorial section. The *Hartford Courant* is America's oldest newspaper in continuous publication. It devoted a full page to a sweeping indictment of Generation X and its noninvolvement in the political process. Bill Clinton was about to trounce Bob Dole. It seemed that the Xers (born between 1965 and 1984) did not vote or donate its resources at the same level the Boomers did (born between 1945 and 1964) when they first got involved in politics.

The implied laziness part bothered me. We had thirty Xers working at our agency at the time, and none were lazy. I asked our research department to review the voting habits of Generation X. Our research department checked. All the factors seemed equal on a per capita basis. Xers did vote. They did contribute to their political parties and they did participate in government. There were just fewer of them. In other words, the young Generation X voters actually cast fewer votes than the young Boomers when they were the same age not because they were lazy but because they were simply a smaller group.

Was this simple difference in the size of the Boomer generation and Generation X the answer to the motorcycle mystery? I reviewed U.S. Census Bureau data to find out, and indeed there were a lot fewer of them—11 percent fewer. There were 78 million Boomers and only 69 million Xers.

That moment of recognition changed my thinking from that point forward. Large and small generations, alternately moving and aging through the marketplace, determine many a company's success or failure. That moment changed the way I counsel my client companies. It spawned the shape of my public presentations. It gave birth to this book.

The core idea of this book is quite simple: Smaller generations buy less stuff; larger generations buy more stuff. When a large generation, such as the Boomers, leaves the market and is replaced by a smaller generation, such as Gen Xers, sales are going to drop. Please excuse the fact that I *repeat* this premise throughout my book, but I have found that people (executives, entrepreneurs, salespeople, marketers, advertisers, etc.) just don't accept this clear-cut concept until you beat them over the head with it. My intention is to show how the simple idea of generational size applies to an ever-widening variety of areas and convince readers to recognize it, believe it, and, most important, put it to use.

—Kenneth W. Gronbach

A WORD FROM THE AUTHOR

Opinions differ on the birth dates and age ranges of the various generations. Here's why I use the ranges found in this book:

A traditional view of a generation is roughly twenty years, the time between the birth of the parents and the birth of their offspring. The end of one generation and the start of another can be fuzzy, marked by an amorphous group of "tweeners," who get to choose the generation they want to be in, based on the one that best represents how they think. Remember, demography is akin to macroeconomics, not micro.

When I selected what I considered to be the most accurate generational chronology, I started with what I felt was the best definition of the Baby Boomers and worked out. Boomers, or War Babies as they were once called, began being born in 1945—even as some forces were still fighting—because many soldiers had already returned home. So the Boomer years were 1945 to 1964, or twenty years. This being established, it was easy to align the GI Generation, The Silent Generation, and Generation X into twenty-year segments. The exception is Generation Y, which I believe will end about 2010 at twenty-five years.

Generations share more than chronology. They share life-changing experiences and events that cause them to bond, like the GI Generation. Sometimes, the sheer size of the cohort shapes its personality, like the huge Baby Boomer generation. Even mammoth Generation Y is said to owe its personality to technology and the Internet. Is demography an exact science? No. Can you use demography to make accurate forecasts about commerce, culture, and economics? Absolutely!

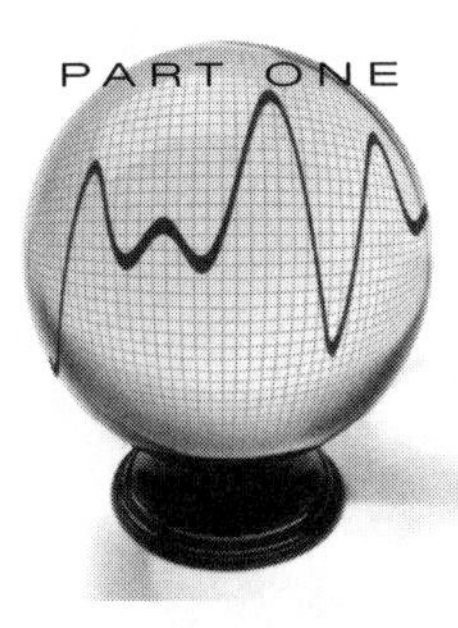

The Parade of Generations

Why Aren't Marketers Paying Attention?

CHAPTER 1

The Generational Impact on Supply and Demand

Everything in business—everything—is affected by supply and demand.

After you determine the product or service you have to sell, you'd better find out who buys what you're selling. Where are the customers? How do you reach them? Above all, are there enough of them? And is their number expanding or shrinking?

Imagine two groups of customers. One has a thousand people and the other has five hundred. Both groups have an identical makeup based on a broad spectrum of characteristics. One group is simply half the size of the other.

Can we make some assumptions about the two groups? Yes we can. Which group will require more food? That's right, the group of one thousand. Which group needs the most diapers as babies? Good. The group of one thousand. Which group buys the most bicycles? Yes, the group of one thousand.

Which group is likely to have more members die in traffic accidents, make the honor roll, or get arrested? The group of one thousand. Which will have more children, build more houses, and have the largest number of hardy elderly who live to be eighty-plus years old? Yes. The one thousand. Why was the answer always the same? *One group is bigger than the other.*

If we prepared the same quantity of food for both groups and then observed the amount left over, we would probably conclude that our group of five hundred was not very hungry. Sound ridiculous? Well, it's what marketers do every day because they don't do the math. When crime went down a few years back, politicians took credit for being "tough on crime." But the truth is that the group from which we draw 65 percent of our criminals, men fifteen to thirty years old, was 11 percent smaller than in the previous twenty years. Simply stated, there were 11 percent fewer crime committers.

In a way I am a victim of my own family's demography. My parents had four boys. I was the youngest and the only Boomer. Our family consumed vast quantities of food. Some of the staples like bread and milk were always in short supply. We all learned that when you sat down at the table you ate and you ate fast, because if you wanted seconds of anything you were going to have to be aggressive.

When my brothers moved out one by one, my mom still cooked the same quantities of food. It was what she was used to. She was on a roll. She couldn't stop. So our table went from scarcity to more than plenty. She was hurt. The family always liked her food; now no one seemed to appreciate it. She would say to me, "Just finish this up." Is it any wonder I ended up the fat kid in the family? My mother had not made adjustments for shifting demography. Marketers do exactly the same thing.

The Generational Parade

Every twenty years or so, the United States creates a new generation. Each generation is bound together by similar wants, needs, motives, and events. As they pass through time, all generations age and consume as they go.

In other words, there's a parade moving through our marketplace. But instead of marching, the parade is aging. This three-dimensional marketing model has generational sections. Those at the front—the oldest—are already disbanding, while the youngest in the back of that parade are just now forming at the fairgrounds. The parade has a pace of its own and we can't slow it down, speed it up, or change the order of each section.

The generational sections vary dramatically in size. This fact makes their consumption habits very predictable. Big ones need more food and bicycles. Little ones will eat and ride less. That's why a graph of U.S. live births is a wavy line, with big generations and small generations taking turns every twenty years.

The field of generational marketing has gained favor in the last ten years or so and many generational-marketing gurus have risen to prominence. Their basic premise is that generations have idiosyncratic personalities that govern their communication and behavior, and that understanding these personalities is imperative to effective marketing. Although I believe this is partially true, I differ strongly on why generations seem to have divergent approaches to life in general and commerce specifically. The gurus would have you believe that they have unlocked the secrets of a particular generation's motives and psyche. For a fee they will share their insights on the special language and secret strategies necessary to sell your product or idea to this generation. It is really not that complex, and for the most part the personality of the generation is determined by something very obvious: its size relative to the generation it follows.

For example, members of Generation X (born 1965 to 1984) were labeled "slackers" and "lazy couch potatoes" because so few Xers responded to help-wanted ads when they entered the entry-level labor force, and the Xers who did respond were said to have a poor attitude and work ethic. Yes, Generation X does have an attitude, but its members are not lazy. People are people. There are simply fewer of them than there are Baby Boomers (born 1945 to 1964)—*nine million fewer, to be exact, or an 11 percent free fall.* For every ten jobs the Boomers left behind, there were only nine Xers to replace them. Job number ten, often a less desirable position like fast-food worker, went begging. In any given workforce there are always 3 or 4 percent who are unemployable. It was this unemployable faction that gave Generation X its undeserved reputation.

Because Generation X is so much smaller than the Boomer generation, it is easy to understand why it is perceived as having an attitude of entitlement. One reason is that the Boomer generation established the public-school infrastructure in the United States by virtue of its mass, and right on its heels came the much smaller Generation X. Imagine the dilemma of all the high school football coaches who were accustomed to selecting only the best athletes from the sea of Boomer tryouts when barely enough Gen Xers showed up to populate the offensive and defensive teams. Even poorly skilled Gen Xers made the team because they were in demand.

Put yourself in the place of smug college recruiters who routinely turned away Boomers who were good students but simply were not the best and the brightest. Along comes Generation X and the recruiters were challenged with filling seats—so standards plunged.

Generation X has not had a problem finding work either. Ten Baby Boomers graduate from entry-level work and there are only nine Generation Xers to fill the jobs. So everybody gets hired. Even when they get fired, Xers have no problem getting hired again.

So does being in demand precipitate an attitude? Yes. Employers have told me that Generation Xers don't like to work. My answer is, "They don't have to."

A very similar thing happened to the Silent Generation at the end of WWII. As the huge GI Generation (born between 1905 and 1924) retired from the military in force, the anemic Silent Generation coursed through the ranks to higher offices at breakneck speed and record time. The Silent Generation had very young officers who were very full of themselves. Some have said that as Generation X and the Silent Generation advanced through the public and private sectors, their abilities were never questioned.

Discovering a Generation's Personality

The principle of supply and demand can play out in many directions and give you the real secrets to understanding a generation's personality. It is very simple really.

As shown in Figure 1.1, there are five distinct generations alive in the United States today. Only two can yield worthwhile returns on a marketer's investment because they follow small generations and therefore spawn expanding markets. These two are the seventy-eight million Baby Boomers and the soon-to-be one hundred million Echo Boomers, or Gen Y. Both of these generations lack an adequate infrastructure to serve their changing needs, whether it is retail, social, legal, or health care.

Marketers seem to miss the fact that generation size is also market size. And marketers don't notice that aging and

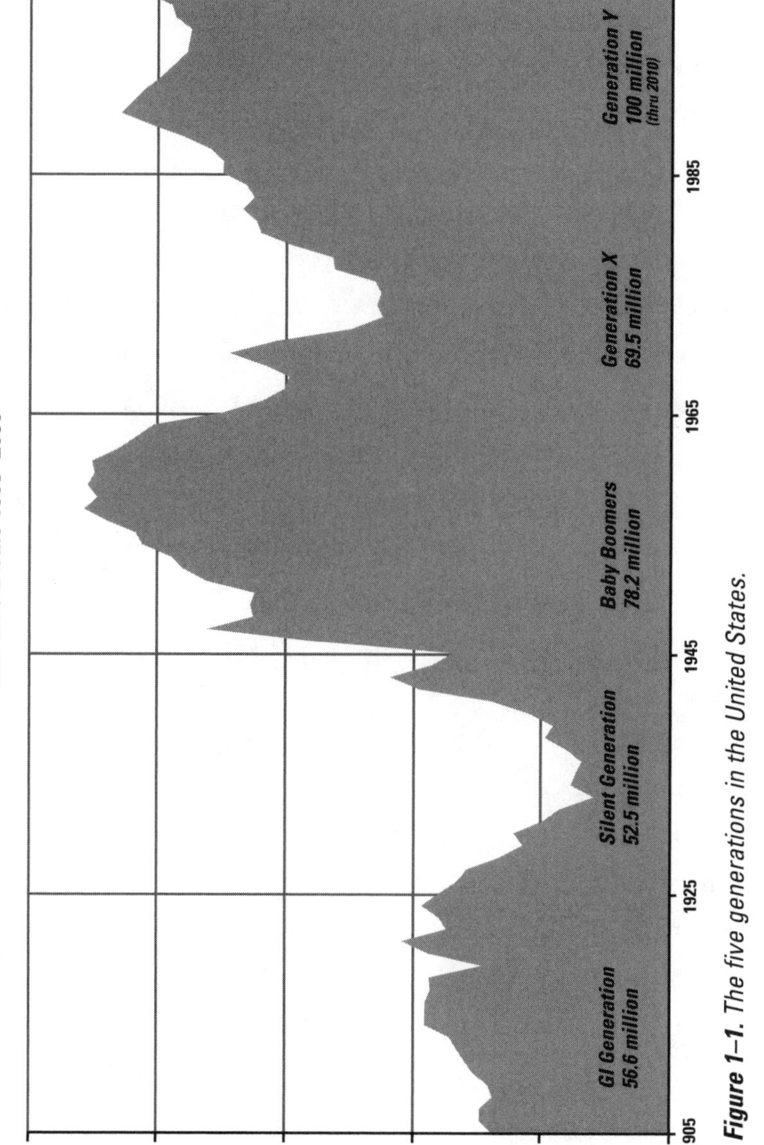

Figure 1–1. *The five generations in the United States.*

generational movement are absolutely consistent. We can't speed them up and we can't slow them down. Each market has a sweet spot or "Best Customer" that sustains a business. As customers grow up, a smart marketer will stay in front of them—and their money.

It is apparent in figure 1.1 that when it comes to business, there are generations of opportunity as well as generations to avoid. Let's say for example that you are General Motors and your obvious goal is to sell new cars to the American market. You know that statistically the ages of your best customers fall into a bell-shaped curve spanning about twenty years, with its peak between forty and forty-five years old. This makes sense because the family car sees the most action during this age. Think about it. The average age at which we get married in the United States is between twenty-five and thirty years old. Assuming that we start our families right away, we can look forward to ferrying teenagers to and from events throughout our forties, and particularly in our early forties. More miles mean more new cars.

Now look at Figure 1.1 again. Do you see a problem? Unless you are blindfolded, you would realize that the Baby Boomers are about to exit your market and you have a serious issue. Gulp. Has Detroit on the whole addressed this issue? No. Is Detroit experiencing serious sales declines? Yes. I guess it's the blindfold.

CHAPTER 2

Who Are These People?

Here's a sketch of each section of the generational parade moving through our marketplace. These summaries are a start. You'll get to know them better as you read more of this book.

The GI Generation

Between 1905 and 1924, there were 56.6 million live births in the United States. Immigration augmented this population. By the end of this twenty-year period, 13.8 million people had come here from Europe, bringing the total to 70.4 million.

This generation "peaked" in volume around 1921. (In other words, the largest number of GI-Generation births in one year occurred in 1921.) The GI Generation is defined by the Great Depression and its participation in World War II. Only a few of these folks—fewer than five million women and men—are still "in the parade."

The GI Generation is the oldest living generation in the United States. This is significant because this generation amassed enormous personal wealth—nearly $11 trillion. They were savers who did not live above their means. The GI Generation left $7 trillion to $10 trillion to their Boomer kids, who will spend it rather than save it. The remaining hardy GI Generation members are still influential because they hold board seats in major corporations and have significant wealth. The wealthy tend to live the longest because they get the best health care. This group was instrumental in electing George Bush in 2000 and 2004. Their influence is dying, so I predict George Bush will likely be our last conservative president until further notice.

One of the hallmarks of this generation was bigotry—big-time bigotry. Racial minorities and women in general suffered considerable oppression at the hands of this generation. At the end of WWII the GI Generation oddly forgave the Germans but maintained a deep-seated resentment of the Japanese because of their treatment of U.S. prisoners and other war crimes. Until just recently it was a very rare thing indeed to see an elderly person driving a Japanese car. The remaining GI Generation survivors are eighty-four and over. The Silents don't harbor this resentment because they did not experience WWII firsthand. They routinely drive Toyotas.

The Silent Generation

Only 52.5 million live births were recorded between 1925 and 1944. The members of this generation—the "Silents"—are currently sixty-four to eighty-three years old. Immigration numbers were actually negative during some of these years (that is, more people left than came in); the total number of immigrants coming to the United States during this period was a paltry 2.4 million because it was a bad idea to come here during the Great Depression. After all, it was just as easy to starve in Europe, and World War II made immigration impossible.

The Silent Generation is the smallest generation of the last century, and it lived in the shadow of the GI Generation. The Silents would hear the war stories, but they couldn't tell any. Ironically, it's as if people forgot the Korean War despite the fierceness of the battles and the suffering of the soldiers and civilians. I don't know why.

This is the generation that will shut down the assisted-living industry as we know it. Just as the hardy remnants of the huge GI Generation gave us the false impression that we are all going to live past 100, the hardy part of this tiny generation will give us the false impression that the trend in longevity has reversed. Once the remainder of the GI Generation is gone, the Silent Generation, with its diminutive presence, will take over the "elderly" position and hold it for twenty years. We will wonder where the old people went.

The Baby Boom Generation

The GI Generation and many of the Silent Generation gave birth to the Baby Boomers, who were born between 1945 and 1964. They were also called "War Babies," because the men returning from WWII really missed their wives and sweethearts. The Boomer birth peak came in 1957 with 4.3 million live births. More people were born in 1957 than in any other year in the history of our nation.

This peak birth year was a full twelve years after the war ended, stretching the "it's so good to be home" theory to its logical limits. One could argue that the war did more than delay the birth peak of this generation. If anything, it might have become bigger without the war. The ranks of the Boomers swelled to nearly eighty million, and marketers have bet everything on the abiding presence of this huge, actively consuming market. However, many forget it is aging and moving forward in the parade.

The Boomers wanted to change the world, and they almost did. But hey, it isn't over yet. Forty or so years ago Boomers wanted to burn down the universities. Now they run them, and the transfer of power has been fairly recent.

That's why I think we will see some changes. For example, Boomers are surprisingly intolerant of those who don't think like them, especially those Boomers who lean hard to the left. As conservatism begins to take a backseat, I believe you will start seeing strong opposition to the religious right, especially in education. We are starting to see Boomer-controlled local, state, and federal government. Yes, marijuana will be legal very soon. What we will see with the Boomers is a manifestation of the Golden Rule: Once the Boomers have all the gold, they will make the rules.

In 2008 we will elect our first real Boomer president. Bill Clinton was not a Boomer president because Boomer money did not put him in office. George Bush is definitely not a Boomer president—GI Generation oil money put him in office.

Generation X

The Silent Generation and many of the Boomers begat the Xers, born between 1965 and 1984.

Generation X is unfairly maligned because pundits miss the point; they don't do their math. *There are 11 percent fewer Gen Xers than Boomers.* Yet they attended college at the rate of 500 per thousand compared to the Boomers at 250 per thousand. When this generation progressed through the public school system, 10 to 15 percent of public schools in the United States closed because of the dramatic drop in enrollment compared with the Boomers. When the Xers entered college, enrollment actually went up. This is noteworthy, especially when evaluating Generation X's qualitative attributes.

Generation X numbers only 69.5 million, and members of this generation have extremely favorable employment prospects in the decades to come. Again, in many categories, for every ten jobs the Boomers exit, there are nine Xers waiting to be fought over.

It might be called "The Strange Career of Generation X." Wherever Gen X goes, things happen and experts are vexed. Career marketers are still baffled by this generation's diminutive consumption. *They are nine million fewer than the Boomers who march before them. Nine million fewer! Eleven percent smaller!* You can repeat this until you are blue in the face, and smart people won't listen or, worse, can't hear you. I can't imagine the number of advertising agency people who have been fired because they just couldn't stimulate this group to consume at the level of the Boomers. What part of *smaller* do they not understand? Gen Xers are not buying enough SUVs from Detroit and the housing market is tanking because Xers don't have the critical mass to buy up the Boomers' starter castles. Just wait until it's the Xers turn to pay the heavy taxes. They won't be able to. I wonder where we will get the money to run the country. Xers will also torpedo private shared-risk health insurance, big-box retailers, and Social Security. On top of creating all this carnage, Generation Xers are arrogant.

Generation Y

This generation of what will be 100 million people represents massive opportunity for marketers. Anyone born between 1985 and 2010 is, and will be, part of Generation Y. This group will stretch the twenty-year pattern of the past four generations to a full twenty-five years. Pregnancy postponements; second and third marriages; and the wonders of drugs like Viagra, Cialis, and Levitra have produced older parents. (If there were ever a match of product and market, it's the Baby Boomer and erectile-dysfunction drugs.)

Much of Gen Y has Boomer parents, but children that older Xers beget now also add to the ranks. Gen Y has an appetite for consumption that is five times stronger than its parents' generations. Just look in their toy boxes. Over a third of them have four parents and eight grandparents. Driven for some reason by guilt—perhaps because they feel that the kids have unduly suffered or they can't spend time with their kids because of custody arrangements—these extended families lavish gifts on the kids. As you learn to consume, you tend to consume.

Because of their massive numbers and the small infrastructure left behind by the Xers, this generation will need to create its own world and compete for everything just as the Boomers did. Its members will of necessity become entrepreneurs and start a sea of small businesses to meet their own needs—just as the Boomers did. They are already redefining the automobile (small, powerful Asian-car hot rods). As a homegrown labor force of epic size, they will stop immigration cold and even restore manufacturing. It was the paltry Generation X that drove manufacturing offshore. Generation Y will bring it back. Generation Y is already filling the nation's technical schools with its best and brightest.

And remember, there's no such thing as a "good" generation or a "bad" one. These are just people aging along in a parade. Their consistent, predictable movement shows us that crime will go up when a large generation occupies the crime-committing age and down when a small generation has its turn in the corresponding criminal sweet spot. But percentages are almost always the same. It's only the population total within certain age parameters that shifts.

I call it the two-percent rule: Two percent do the work; two percent cause the trouble; the rest eat the food.

> *"Two percent do the work; two percent cause the trouble; the rest eat the food."*

CHAPTER 3

Bell Curves, Pies, and Your "Best Customer"

The customer who sustains your business has a static description. For Japanese motorcycles, the description is a sixteen- to twenty-four-year-old male. Problems occur because the actual customer is a real person. He or she is aging in the parade passing through your marketplace and is therefore not static. Maybe we don't think about aging because it is so slow.

Along with everyone else on the generational parade route, your customer today will be somewhere else in the years ahead. His or her wants and needs today can be very different five years from now. Your success depends on whether there are an increasing number of bodies in the population aging and moving toward the static description of your customer or aging and moving away from it.

Finding the Automotive Sweet Spot

Consider the automobile market. Ford, General Motors, and Chrysler have been selling record numbers of cars—especially the very profitable sport-utility vehicles (i.e., trucks with nice upholstery)—to the Baby Boomers. However, the bloom is off the rose because *Boomers are aging out of their peak car-buying years at the rate of one every eight seconds.*

Detroit's car-buying sweet spot is a bell-shaped curve representing customers between thirty-five and forty-five years old; it peaks in the early forties. Boomers are now age forty-four to sixty-three. I am imagining the dialog in a boardroom at Ford: "Our customer has naturally aged out of our market. Does anyone see a problem here? No? Good. Well, let's build them some more SUVs and see if our advertising agency can stimulate sales."

As described in detail in chapter 4, Detroit should be focusing on Generation Y—the generation whose peak car-buying years are ahead of it—instead of the departing Boomers.

Businesses would understand their markets better if they would simply determine who their best customers are and match those customers with the *demographic peak* of the market they seek—the top of the birthrate bell curve for that generation.

> *"Ideally your product's best-customers are eight to ten years younger than the corresponding peak in the population, generation, or market you are pursuing. This way your best-customer market will naturally age toward you while increasing in size."*

The optimal position is in front of the curve. Ideally your product's best-customers are eight to ten years younger than the corresponding peak in the population, generation, or market you are pursuing. This way your best-customer market will naturally age toward you while increasing in size. The front of the bell curve is also what is called "the expanding pie" market.

Expanding-pie markets are infinitely easier to work with than their shrinking-pie-market counterparts. In an expanding market, a product or service sells based on merit and value—not on price. In expanding markets, you can be creative and independent. You can take chances, make mistakes, and still make a lot of money. Shrinking markets reduce products and services to commodities sold only on price and with skinny margins.

It is a mystery to me why so many businesspeople don't know if their markets are shrinking or expanding. To me this is irresponsible management. Shrinking markets only get worse. Expanding markets only get better. Why are so many businesses content to be mired in shrinking markets?

Cell Phones: The Market That Keeps Expanding!

I am an early adopter. I like to have cool new things before other people. My first mobile phone in the eighties was the size of a bread box (well, not quite). It had a strap and you could wear it over your shoulder. It had a big heavy battery and a handset from a home phone. Wherever I went, interest in the phone was intense. I knew this phone thing was going to be big. Talk about an expanding market. Mobile phones morphed into car phones, and car phones morphed into cell phones. Today my cell phone is about the same size as my Volvo key. Every member of my family has one and would be lost without it.

My teenage Generation Y daughters use their phones to take photos, look at photos, send photos, make videos, look at videos, send videos, text with their friends, listen to music, play games, calculate, get news, tell time, e-mail, plan, view a calendar, take notes, set alarms, get voice mail, leave voice mail, and *make telephone calls.*

If ever there was a well-positioned product category it is the cell phone. Boomers have inhaled them and use them, but members of Generation Y have integrated them into their very beings and play them like musical instruments. The phone manufacturers and attendant phone services continue to ride the crest of these two huge markets by continuously reinventing themselves and making getting a new phone every two years mandatory. I don't know where it will end.

The marketing of cell phones and cell service is marketing genius. We don't actually buy the phones, or so we think. The purchase is buried in the cost of the service contract, giving us the impression that the phones are free. The phones are actually quite expensive when bought separately, a fact that should give us an idea of how little it costs to provide cell service. Cell service providers like Verizon and Cingular spend hundreds of millions of dollars on marketing and advertising. This is a sign of business health.

There is an important exception to the generational-marketing rule of staying ahead of the wave. Small markets like Generation X, the Silent Generation, and the remnant of the GI Generation can be profitable if you have a brand-new product preferably in a brand-new category (that is, a product without any history). But if you have been selling a product to the Boomers (such as beer, for example) and they age out of their high demand for your product, you will definitely be disappointed by Generation X's demand. However, say you have discovered a new beverage that for some reason is very appealing to thirtysomethings and has no sales history. You could be quite content with the sales figures generated by the Generation X market.

There is no question that if you introduced your beverage when the Boomers were in their twenties and thirties you would have sold more, but hey, ignorance is bliss. If you discovered a pharmaceutical that could add ten years to a geriatric's life span, you can be sure you would sell a ton of it to the remnants of the GI Generation and the Silent Generation even if they are small, declining markets for almost everything else. Small markets can be healthy markets if you have a brand-new product.

However, for my money, use the U.S. Census birth charts to find the expanding market you want to sell to and stay on its front side. It's a lot more fun.

CHAPTER 4

Case Study

Detroit, Japan, and the Best Customers for Cars

There is nothing more pathetic than watching a consumer-goods or durable-goods giant circle the drain when its sales go south. No one ever fixes the problem. Everyone wants to fix the blame instead. Detroit's red ink, for example, is a tragic by-product of the quarterly report and the total lack of vision it precipitates. You cannot be a visionary by thinking three months into the future. If Detroit would pay attention to the demographics of car buying—and to the parade of generations marching through the car market—it could stop the annual flow of red ink.

The best customer for a new American car, after all, is a forty-three-year-old male. This customer buys more new cars than anyone else. His new-car buying years are best between the ages of thirty-three and fifty-three, with the peak being forty-three.

This peak is significant for the Boomer generation, which peaked in 1957 with over 4.3 million live births. Figure 1.1 demonstrated that the years 1957 to 1961 perched high and in the middle of the huge Boomer bell curve. These significant five years define Boomers' impact on any market they encounter.

In the case of the automobile market, the last of the Boomer men born during the five peak years turned forty-three in 2004. At that point a dramatic decline in the sale of new American cars began. Annual new-car sales now range from sixteen to eighteen million.

Foreign car manufacturers seem to understand this significant five years in the Boomer bell curve. Yet Detroit has been slow to see the inevitability of its effect on the new-car market. The car market's future is Generation Y, now under twenty-four years old.

Generation Y's predecessor, Generation X, has vexed Detroit car manufacturers and their advertising agencies. American car manufacturers want desperately to have this group match the sales levels of the Baby Boomers, but all efforts thus far have been unsuccessful. I think at some level Detroit may be taking this failure personally, thinking that Generation X is holding back its car-buying dollars until

Detroit asks for them in just the right way. Then Generation X will release its presumed pent-up demand.

I have watched the different advertising pitches and television campaigns over the years and sensed the increasing desperation and frustration in squeezing better sales out of Generation X. Enough already! *Generation X will never be able to buy at the level of the Boomers because it is a smaller generation. It has nine million fewer people.* So if Generation X's new-car sales are "off" by millions of cars, this is probably why. The best course for car makers is to think less about Generation X and focus more on Generation Y. I know I am being far too simplistic and a bit mean-spirited, but stay with me.

Consider Toyota. Toyota gets it. Toyota made a long-term investment of time, money, and effort to find out what kind of car Generation Y wants. Keep in mind that Gen Y is only twenty-three years old and under in 2008. It is, however, consuming at a rate that is 500 percent higher than its Boomer parents in adjusted dollars age for age, and there are already more than eighty million of them. This is *the* emerging and expanding market for automobiles.

The peak age on Gen Y's bell curve is currently eighteen. Toyota and other Asian brands took a good look at how these kids were modifying and customizing their own cars. They then translated this intelligence to their production lines and produced cars that Gen Y is now inhaling. Detroit, on the other hand, did not take this market seriously until about two years ago. Maybe it's because you don't see any Gen Ys customizing

SUVs or big pickups. Because Detroit is off to such a slow start, Asian manufacturers have an enormous head start marketing to Gen Y.

The movie *The Fast and the Furious* reflects this generation's automotive tastes, but another excellent way to determine what kinds of new cars will sell is to look at the used cars kids are driving now and how they have modified them. They are telling auto manufacturers what they want. Lee Iacocca watched what young people were doing to customize their rides in the late fifties and early sixties. Back then, kids wanted lightweight, sporty, high-performance cars they could afford. Lee gave them the Ford Mustang and they inhaled it. Detroit could replicate that success today if it would just pay attention.

Generation Y wants reliable, small, lightweight cars that are fuel efficient, high-tech, fast, powerful, and very cool. They must have unique ground effects, spoilers, exotic paint, very-low-profile tires, and trick wheels. Kids like options and choices—who doesn't? Detroit needs to let young people build their own new cars. Gen Y will actually buy more new cars than the Boomers and it will buy them at an earlier age. What an opportunity for Detroit to turn things around!

Oh, I almost forgot! One of Detroit's biggest assets is the fact that American cars are just that—American cars. The GI Generation was very loyal to Detroit because of WWII. Sure, some did buy European cars, especially Mercedes, but it was a rare thing to see a driver from the GI Generation in a Japanese car. Members of this generation disliked the Germans intensely—until the war was over. They hated the Japanese because of the way they treated allied prisoners of war. The GI Generation took this bias to the grave. Now when you see elderly people driving Toyotas, you can say with reasonable certainty that they are Silents born after 1925. The Silent Generation did not fight in WWII.

The marketer's challenge will be dealing with that interval between the falloff in new-car sales to Boomers and Gen Y sales kicking in. Remember, the "peak" of Gen Y is currently about eighteen years old. The interval could be as long as ten years. Gulp!

Of course, outside influences can change the description of the best new-car customer. A gas shortage or a serious spike in prices could have an impact. It would force the Boomers out of their historic buying habits and gas-guzzling SUVs and into smaller, more economical cars. Alternative-fuel mandates could really turn things upside down, too.

Oil and the Generations

Ironically, Detroit could catch a break from the Organization of the Petroleum Exporting Countries (OPEC). There are thirteen members of OPEC, and most of them are in the Middle East. Collectively they supply about 40 percent of the world's oil. When you supply 40 percent of a market you control the market and set the prices.

One time at a gas station, a woman pulled in next to me with a Cadillac SUV on steroids. To me a Cadillac SUV is a contradiction. She looked a little on the edge, like someone who was about to experience pain and knew it. I asked, "Are you sure you want to do this?" I watched the color drain from her face as she pumped the gas. I asked her if she was going to be ok. She said yes, and I left. She is probably still there.

Higher prices at the pump ultimately produce a different mind-set among drivers and home owners who heat with oil. It makes them start to think. They think about smaller, more efficient cars. They think about dependence on OPEC oil. They think about alternative fuels for their cars and their homes. They think about driving less and traveling less. They think about conserving, polluting less, and global warming. Some even think about changing their positions on offshore drilling and atomic energy. They think about how ridiculous it is to depend on fire and fossil fuels to get us around and keep us warm. They also think about how angry they are getting because this mysterious OPEC group they don't know or understand is squeezing them. Anger is good. Anger produces change, invention, and innovation.

OPEC does not want us to think any of these things. It only has one product: oil. If we reduce our consumption of the product, OPEC makes less money. OPEC hates that. So it prefers to keep prices just below where we start to think and start to get angry. I forecast that OPEC, to keep Americans from getting angry and moving away from fossil fuel, will have to dramatically reduce its price per barrel of oil and keep it there for a few years. This will be good for Detroit. It will buy some time, some wiggle room. If this happens, Detroit should seize the opportunity and innovate like there is no tomorrow. This way it can prepare for Generation Y. Generation Y will not tolerate a dependence on fossil fuel and fire to get around and stay warm.

An Idea from Porsche

What else can Detroit do to capture the Gen Y car buyer? One suggestion is to take a page from Porsche.

I am a Porsche nut. I have been blessed with the wherewithal to own several of them in my lifetime. Although the car is universally recognized, it doesn't really have a broad market appeal and is not all that easy to sell when you want to move up to a new one. It's not the kind of car you trade in at the dealer, because you can always get more money if you sell it privately (but a private sale is not always easy).

About twenty years ago I saw a Porsche ad in a major enthusiasts' magazine. The ad encouraged people to buy *used* Porsches. It was not a dealer ad. It was from Porsche of America. I thought it was curious because Porsche of America did not sell used Porsches. But the more I thought about it, I realized the genius of the concept. Porsche of America depended on the sale of used Porsches to sell its new Porsches. A healthy used-Porsche market increased the trade-in value of

Porsches overall and fostered new-car sales. The people who bought the used Porsches were a ready market for new Porsches down the road. It's a real win/win.

There is a moral here: If you want to grow your market, get entry-level buyers to buy your used cars. That will keep your new cars selling because dealers will be able to offer more for the trade-ins due to the high demand for used cars. In addition you will have a ready crop of new-car buyers when your entry-level buyers age. Generation Y is currently buying and driving new and used Asian cars with a vengeance. Detroit has a problem.

Detroit needs to get a handle on shrinking and expanding markets. It's really economics 101. The Boomer market for cars is shrinking and will never expand again. *Generation X is nine million people smaller than the Baby Boomer generation and can never consume at the Baby Boomer level no matter how much marketing money is wasted trying to make them do so. The Gen Y market is expanding and will continue to expand for the next thirty years.* Is there any mystery as to which one of these markets is the future?

Is Detroit history? No. But it will take a backseat to Asian cars for a while. Toyota will be the sales leader. Honda won't be far behind. The dramatic drop in sales of American cars will be the Pearl Harbor we need to wake up and take this issue seriously. Detroit will gradually shut down the assembly lines for the gas-guzzling, behemoth SUVs as money and the unions allow. It will retool and begin to build powerful, lightweight, economical cars that are right for the new market. Alternative-energy cars will be important to Detroit as well. We are very good at technology; in fact most other nations steal it from us.

Remember what Admiral Isoroku Yamamoto said after his attack on Pearl Harbor: "I fear all we have done is to awaken a sleeping giant and fill him with a terrible resolve."

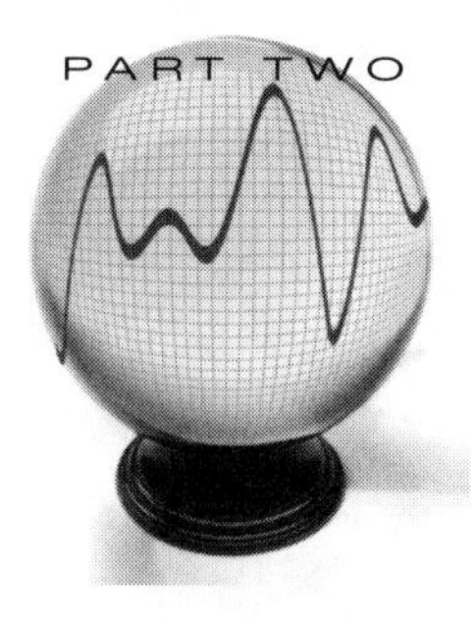

PART TWO The Older Generations

CHAPTER 5

Silent Virtues

A Small Group with Its Own Impact

I grew up in the world of the war story. Kids love to hear war stories.

"Sarge" was a friend of my Mom's. He had been in a tank in Europe in WWII. The tank took a direct hit from something that crippled it—and him. He lived, but apparently his crew died around him. He could tell the story in tragic detail, and while he spoke you could hear a pin drop. Sarge was a musician prior to the war but could no longer play. He just drank.

My friend's dad was in the U.S. Air Force toward the end of the war, when we were firebombing Japan. His description of the flack that they had to fly through was so real that you felt like you were there. He said there was so much firepower on the ground that the Japanese would simply point their anti-aircraft guns up and fire them continuously, forcing the bombers to fly through the hail of ordinance.

My girlfriend's dad gave an account of the ground war in Germany, where he jumped into a foxhole face-to-face with a very frightened young German soldier. It was kill or be killed. He remembered the look on the soldier's face.

Our pastor was a tail gunner on a B-52 over Germany. It deeply troubled him to shoot down enemy planes. But he did. Tail gunners as a rule did not last very long, so our pastor, as he tells it, made a deal with God: If God would get him through the war, he would devote his life to God as a pastor. God kept his part of the deal and so did our pastor.

You can't make up stories like these, but I am sure people tried.

The Truth About Silents

Think about it. If you were born between 1925 and 1944 you are currently approximately sixty-four to eighty-three years old. You missed World War II, but not by much. But a miss is as good as a mile when it comes to wars. Your overall numbers are small and your generation is referred to as Silent, presumably because you have little to say and are therefore reticent. Just between you and me, I think history dealt you a bad hand. When I think of Silents, I think of insurance salesmen with Rotary pins.

The Silent generation numbered 52.5 million—the smallest generation of the past 100-plus years. It is a dubious distinction. But what about the virtues of the Silent Generation? In that regard, the Silent Generation was essentially a small echo of the GI Generation. Silents drove the same cars as members of the GI Generation. They wore the same clothes. They enjoyed the same music and art. They drank together. They had the same work ethic. They were the same, only smaller.

The only thing Silents didn't have in common with the GI Generation was the fact that they didn't fight in World War II. WWII is a defining event of the past 100 years, and it wasn't given to the Silents. They listened to stories; they couldn't tell them. This made them Silent.

It's true that many Silents fought in the Korean War. But as wars go, the Korean conflict bore little resemblance to WWII. WWII was just that, a world war. The allied forces and the millions of men all over the world who volunteered to fight against the tyranny of Germany and Japan clearly saw the lines between good and evil, right and wrong. The allies had to win WWII or the world would be a very different place.

The Korean conflict, on the other hand, was simply a localized civil war fueled by the United States and the Soviet Union. No one "won" the Korean Conflict, and this begged the question about why we got involved in the first place. This war was not popular. It is a war that the United States preferred to forget, and hence it became known as "The Forgotten War."

Large generations dwarf the small generations that follow. The Silent Generation, as with Generation X later, lives in the wake of an enormous generation. This fact precipitates some givens, such as less consumption and little competition for employment. In the Silents' case, the war-story issue further exacerbates their "silence." The Korean War and Vietnam did not level the playing field.

The Challenge of Marketing to Silents

Of all the miscalculations that occur regarding generations, Silents are miscalculated most often. Fortunately, with the exception of the assisted-living industry and retirement homes, those miscalculations have had the least consequence. Yet marketers can look at this "dip" in live births and learn from it.

For example, Jeb Bush, the brother of President George W. Bush and former governor of Florida, was concerned about ten years ago that retirees no longer favored Florida as the place to enjoy their later years. It seems that retirement communities were seeing a serious drop-off in new arrivals and Jeb was rightfully concerned. He speculated that Arizona was offering a better deal, so he appointed a blue-ribbon panel of experts to research just where these turncoats were going. Jeb wanted Florida to reverse the attrition. Florida, after all, needs retirees to make ends meet, along with orange juice sales and spring break revenues.

So what did the blue-ribbon panel find? It found that retirees were in fact making their way to Arizona and elsewhere, but there was no way to prove that they were defectors who should have settled in Florida. And besides, Arizona had its own problems with the slow growth of new retirees. An Arizona panel was probably investigating Florida.

Both committees could have checked the census data—the same data that supplied the information for Figure 1.1—and they would have realized that a very low birthrate and virtually no immigration between 1925 and 1944 precipitated a deficit in the U.S. population. This deficit came right on the heels of the birth and immigration surge of the GI Generation. It is a study in contrasts.

Can you profitably market to the Silent Generation? Of course you can. This generation is currently (as of this writing) sixty-four to eighty-three years old. There are products that this group will buy that are historically representative of the needs of this demographic. They include food, clothing, housing, medical products, medical services, medicines, entertainment, recreation, financial services, transportation, and communications. Savvy marketers will recognize that this age group has very deep pockets for any product that will help them maintain their independence and stay in their own homes. Companies like StairGlide have made millions manufacturing chairs that transport people up and down stairs. I can remember how relieved my grandmother was when I installed handles that enabled her to get in and out of the tub. The list goes on and on: scooters, automatic doors, medical alerts that are worn around the neck. Don't forget cell phones and personal computers. And here's a true story: I have a friend who installed an automatic garage door opener for his two elderly aunts and, as a result, he was the only family member mentioned in their wills.

Just remember: If you are a marketer focusing on the Silent Generation, you need to be aware that this generation is a very small group following the very large GI Generation. The commercial infrastructure necessary to serve this group is probably overbuilt and will need to shrink before the infrastructure and the size of the Silent market match. In short, it is going to be hard to make money with this group. I would move on to something else if I could.

> *"The only thing Silents didn't have in common with the GI Generation was the fact that they didn't fight in World War II. WW II is a defining event of the past 100 years, and it wasn't given to the Silents. They listened to stories; they couldn't tell them. This made them Silent."*

CHAPTER 6

Case Study

How the "Graying Of America" Myth Will Take Down the Assisted-Living Industry

> Baseball is like so much else in life. It's like voting, dating, parenting, dieting: Gut feelings, myth, lore and assumption carry more weight than black-and-white facts. We want to believe what we want to believe . . . . Against all reason and all objective evidence, it feels like the right thing to do.
>
> —Joan Ryan, *San Francisco Chronicle*, May 6, 2004

Imagine an Antarctic explorer driven by the desire to be first to the South Pole. He accounted for everything and chose the best men, provisions, and equipment. He listened to the experts, researched the failed attempts of his predecessors, and found the best advice on weather. He was prepared. The expedition sailed as far as it could before the men set out on foot.

They were dressed properly and had plenty of food and supplies. They had a clear objective: to reach the South Pole by heading due south. Morale was high on the first day and progress was theirs. They pushed on as long as possible, then stopped to set up camp.

But our seasoned explorer was startled in the morning when he took a compass reading as the expedition was about to break camp. Due south had moved.

Before turning in the night before, he made a mental note of distant ice formations that would guide them as they set out the next day. Now, according to his compass and the ice formation, they were a full fifteen degrees off course.

He was baffled. He decided not to tell his men until the problem with the compass was corrected. But there was no solution. The compass continued to show a counterintuitive heading and, worse yet, the heading continued to change. Our seasoned explorer was distraught.

Some time later, using stellar navigation, he determined that the party was thirty miles from where he knew they actually were. What was going on?

He finally confessed to members of his expedition that they were lost. Fear, discouragement, and frustration coursed though the group like wildfire. To exacerbate the situation further, they discovered after crossing their own tracks that they were going in circles. The expedition failed and the men nearly perished.

Our leader had not taken into consideration that the solid ice beneath their feet was actually an ice floe. He never considered the most obvious explanation. He never trusted his counterintuitive tool, the compass.

Are we so unlike our Antarctic explorer? We resist change. We project the present infinitely into the future. We see what we want to see. And that's ok? No. People age and grow old and that's ok. As they age they change, and the changes are very predictable. Our ice floe is time. Trust your calendar.

"Our leader had not taken into consideration that the solid ice beneath their feet was actually an ice floe. He never considered the most obvious explanation. He never trusted his counterintuitive tool, the compass."

The Myth of the Graying of America

An example of just how far off course our collective thinking can go is found in the myth of "The Graying of America."

About ten years ago I attended a symposium on aging, which was sponsored by a major metropolitan newspaper. The panel of speakers prattled on about how the elderly were going to overrun the United States. Experts waxed eloquent about the design and layout of cities to accommodate the heavy wheelchair traffic. Doorways would be wider and curbs would need to be ramped. Apartments would all be one level and elevators would abound. I tried to picture *elderly sidewalk* rage as the sea of chrome wheelchairs jockeyed for position and waited for the walk light. (By the way, would they change the walk light and show a glowing symbol of a wheelchair?)

I thought to myself: Who are they talking about? It can't be The GI Generation born between 1905 and 1924, because this generation was fading fast. In fact most of their 75-million-plus members were already dead. *You see, generations don't get bigger as they age, they get smaller.* That's because of the dying part.

They also couldn't be talking about the Silent Generation, those folks born 1925 to 1944. This generation would struggle to fit the GI-Generation footprint because *it had almost twenty million fewer people.* There certainly would be no overrunning from this generation.

Ah, they must be referring to the Boomers born between 1945 and 1964! But wait. Ten years ago Boomers were thirty years away from being elderly, so it couldn't be the Boomers. Just what mystery population is this learned group talking about?

I made a near-fatal error. I raised my hand and asked who exactly these elderly people were who were about to overrun America. Giving the evidence of the oldest three generations, I stated that we are not going to be overrun with elderly, but rather we are going to be running out of elderly. There was a long, stony silence.

Finally after what seemed like an eternity the host and moderator jumped in, looked at me disdainfully and said, "That is precisely why we are having this symposium now, so there is plenty of time to prepare." Everyone was delighted and relieved with this answer and the symposium resumed as before.

The people born at the end of the GI Generation are now about eighty-four years old—well beyond the average life span of seventy-six for women and seventy-two for men. In observing this group, we have empirically concluded that we're all living longer. We have concluded that we're becoming a nation of old people. We have concluded that this elderly market will go on forever.

Don't believe what you see. Do *not* believe what you see. Remember the Antarctic explorer. His eyes saw the distant ice formations and he decided his compass was wrong.

Books on the "age wave" and the "graying of America" have captured our imaginations and marketing plans. And of course, the American Association of Retired Persons (AARP) has much to gain by perpetuating the myth. After all, it is a lobbying force to be reckoned with as long as voters fill its ranks. AARP says you've started to age when you reach forty-five. One publishing authority on aging joked to me that "the AARP will soon be calling twentysomethings 'the real young elderly' and then try to sell them insurance policies." In my opinion, the AARP is most responsible for perpetuating the myth that we are soon going to be overrun with elderly people.

About ten years ago I called the AARP because the executive director at the time, Horace Deets, had stated in the Fall 1998 issue of AARP's *Modern Maturity* magazine that Baby Boomers were turning fifty at the rate of eight per second. The real number is one every eight seconds—or the difference between five billion and eighty million. That's a bit of a spread (4.92 billion) and not an acceptable margin of error. For an esteemed organization, this is pretty reckless.

Mr. Deets did not take my call and I was routed to the head of research. I asked the polite lady there to read the misprint to me out loud. At first, she couldn't see a problem. Then, with some prompting, and after a few moments and a bit of stunned silence, she said, "You'll have to forgive us, we are a little math deprived." I thanked her for making my point and we hung up.

My point—and the point of this book—is the magnitude and consequence of not doing the math as it applies to the generations. This is especially true in business in general and marketing in particular. Calculating how generations affect the U.S. commercial, social, and political marketplace is simple but for some reason it is not easy.

Target audiences, customers, and constituents come from populations of people. We must know and understand the generations that make up these populations as they move through our marketplace. This generational movement determines the only thing that means anything in business: supply and demand. That's why we want our market information to be accurate. We have to be careful where we get it.

The truth about the future elderly population lays with numbers at the U.S. Center for Health Statistics and the U.S. Census Bureau. What we're seeing out there are the healthier, wealthier, last 6 or 7 percent of seventy-five million people. If we believe that this is an expanding market, we'll be just like the Antarctic explorer following the ice formations.

The GI Generation was huge. But most of it isn't here anymore. Its members died. We're seeing the last few million people who are alive from that generation, and we are drawing some very bad conclusions.

Right behind this group is the Silent Generation—the smallest generation of the previous century. This is where we'll get our elderly people for the next twenty years. So for the next two decades it will seem that we are hiding our elderly, when the real answer is that only 52.5 million of them were born in the first place. That's a 25 percent freefall in the size of the elderly market, compared to when the GI Generation occupied the market en force.

Boomers cannot take up the slack by suddenly aging. Age is naturally sequential. The parade has its pace. You can't speed it up, you can't slow it down, and you can't step out of place. Trust the calendar. It's correct.

The Impending Death of Assisted Living

If there is any industry that is refusing to trust the calendar, it is the assisted-living industry. After all, it's easy to see what is going to happen with the future population of America's elderly. As the significant number of elderly from the GI Generation die off, the elderly population will become increasingly made up of the tiny remnants of the Silent Generation for the next twenty years. In other words, there aren't many customers in the generational parade moving toward the assisted-living industry. But don't tell them that!

I live on a two-lane state highway in Connecticut. There are advantages and disadvantages to living on a well-traveled road. One disadvantage is the road noise, but our house is set back far enough so this is not an issue. One serious advantage is the fact that our house gets plowed out first after a snowstorm and is easily accessible by emergency vehicles such as fire trucks and ambulances. This is probably one of the reasons why a man from a neighboring town across the Connecticut River decided to build a huge, modern, assisted-living facility just down the street from me. It seems that he and his family had been in the assisted-living business for generations, and this new facility was to be their crowning achievement.

Our small town was all abuzz because this huge facility would become the largest single entity on our town's grand list. It would pay a lot in taxes and not use the town's services. For example, the new facility would not add any new kids to the school system. However, we were told that there would be a steady stream of ambulances. Because if there is one thing assisted-living customers did on a regular basis, it's die. This nonstop turnover of assisted-living customers makes the business so vulnerable to shifting demography. You really need a steady flow of live customers to keep the business viable.

I read in the newspaper about the plans to build the facility. I mustered the courage to give the owner a call and see if we could have a frank discussion about the future of the assisted-living industry.

The assisted-living industry has grossly overbuilt the rest-home infrastructure in anticipation of a sea of elderly Baby Boomers. The problem is they are twenty years too early, because the Boomers are only about forty-four to sixty-three years old in 2008. No amount of misunderstanding is going to make them any older. In the meantime, the United States will fill the elderly ranks with the members of the Silent Generation, the smallest generation of the last 100 years.

This is why I forecast that the assisted-living industry will be brought to near collapse, not because of rising medical costs, wage increases, or inadequate Medicaid reimbursement, but because there simply will not be enough elderly people to fill the beds. It is a shame no one bothered to check the U.S. Census.

To stay alive, assisted-living facilities will seek to fill their beds with anyone who has a pulse. In a strange way this may be fortuitous because mentally challenged people who once were simply institutionalized in state mental hospitals can now share facilities with the elderly.

There is a problem, however: The two groups are not necessarily homogenous. The elderly typically have diminished physical capacity and the mentally challenged have diminished mental capacity. When conflicts arise, the elderly are no match for their physically stronger counterparts. Don't put your parents in an assisted-living facility that resembles a halfway house. You want their twilight years to be as peaceful as possible. Personally, I will never willingly go into an assisted-living facility.

My conversation with the man who would be my new neighbor and the owner of the new assisted-living facility did not go well. But that was expected. He did not buy into my logic and took everything I said personally. I really don't blame him. I told him that I had warned Marriot Corporation about building assisted-living facilities in Fairfield County, Connecticut, a few years earlier. Marriot took the advice and shut down plans almost overnight once it verified my facts. My prospective new neighbor, however, proceeded to go ahead with his plans. Construction started about three years ago and is now complete. There are no cars in the parking lot, yet. Receivership and other financial issues complicated the process. (Banks know when an industry is going south. They seem to have a sixth sense. Believe me; banks are not math deprived and they understand shifting demography. I still don't like them.)

The assisted-living industry's infrastructure is much larger than it needs to be to serve the Silent Generation. Inventive marketers who find a secondary use for this infrastructure could make themselves wealthy. Meanwhile, owners of assisted-living facilities, Alzheimer's units, retirement communities, and everything geriatric are saying, "Wait a minute! Where'd the elderly go?"

And the answer is: "They were never born."

> *"The assisted-living industry's infrastructure is much larger than it needs to be to serve the Silent Generation . . . . Owners of assisted-living facilities, Alzheimer's units, retirement communities, and everything geriatric are saying, 'Wait a minute! Where'd the elderly go?' And the answer is: 'They were never born.'"*

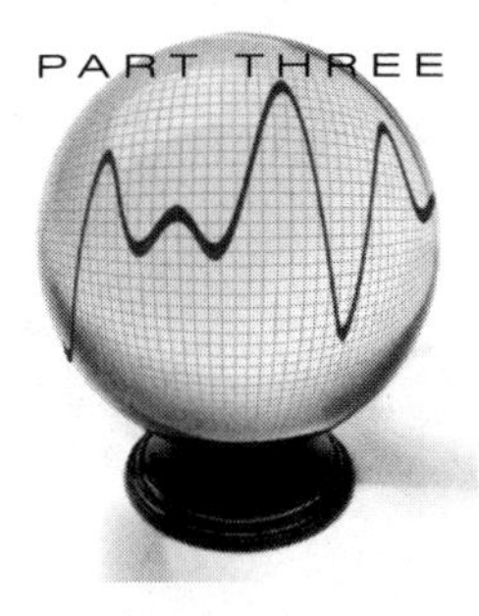

PART THREE

The Baby Boomers

The Radical-Change Generation and Its Impact on Today and Tomorrow

CHAPTER 7

The Boomers
Mass, Money, and Motivation

If Boomers could buy a nuclear submarine and somehow be autonomous, we'd be the second most powerful nation on the planet. Our dynamic power goes beyond sheer mass.

I believe that when the history is written Baby Boomers will take their well-deserved place among the dynamic, historic generations that were agents of change. Media attention to what some did in the 1960s makes us come off as protesters and rebels. But a closer look delivers a richer, more complex interpretation.

We, the Baby Boom Generation (as one of them, I say can

"we"), have invented our own world and began to redefine things in the late sixties and early seventies. We have produced our own music, art, clothing, and literature. We have our own vision. And we still plan to change the world. Our first president from the Boomer generation, Bill Clinton, didn't change the world because his tenure as president was a bit too early to get the full Boomer support necessary. Boomers were not running things yet, but things could very well be different for the next Boomer president.

Why did the Boomers foster such change? People write volumes on this subject, but my short answer comes from the Boomers' place in that generational parade: *We follow the Silent Generation and we dwarf them in size.*

Each generation looks to the previous one for information, similar to the way schoolchildren get their cues from the big kids on the playground. The Silent Generation looked to the GI Generation and copied it. There were a lot of big kids to copy. The Silents adopted their work ethic, their fidelity, and their sense of duty. They adopted their frugal spending habits and their tendency to save money.

When Boomers looked to the Silents, we couldn't see very many. There were no big kids on the playground to copy. So we decided to make things up on our own.

Examination brings perspective on the character of the Boomer as well. We are masters of situational ethics. When we made up our own new world, the elders disapproved. Easily the best way to function under disapproving conditions was defiance. Besides, the elders wouldn't understand, even if they heard the truth. So we lied to our parents. We don't respect authority, and we don't respect the law. In fact, many Boomers thought there was going to be a real revolution especially after the Kent State riots. The saying "All's fair in love and war" is what I call "situational ethics."

Furthermore, having to make it up as we went along, we found that our brave new world required questioning everything our parents stood for, including loyalty, frugality, and trustworthiness. We count up the second, third, and fourth marriages and wonder why others look to us as a generation of people who can't keep their word. Our response is, "I meant it at the time!"

> *"When Boomers looked to the Silents, we couldn't see very many. There were no big kids on the playground to copy. So we decided to make things up on our own."*

Aside from a few character flaws, we're a force to be reckoned with. We have mass and motivation. We spend our money passionately. Spending on our children and grandchildren—a marketer's dream—is happening at an unprecedented level.

When Boomers decide they like something, they don't just buy. They inhale. Take SUVs—just about the stupidest form of transportation on the planet: six thousand pounds of four-wheel drive that you will never need. In reality, these things are nothing more than trucks with a few added bells and whistles. So who benefits by the whole process? Detroit. Trucks are cheap to build. A Ford F-150 pickup costs $20,000. If you decorate it with all the SUV stuff, you'll get $45,000.

But that SUV market will disappear as fast as it arrived. We'll be stuck with all these horrendous trucks. Right now, Boomers are embracing big cars again. Detroit is accommodating them by building big cars with big motors, just like the old days.

Unlike the GI Generation and the Silents who emulated them, Boomers don't spend wisely. They don't save either. But Boomers will inherit more spending money. There may be a lot of poor old people around in twenty years, but for now, we're seeing the greatest transfer of wealth in the history of the world.

To get an idea of the numbers we're talking about, let's take a little math break.

One, Two, Three . . . A Million, A Billion, A Trillion

I don't think most people, especially politicians and newscasters, know the difference between a million, a billion, and a trillion. Try counting softly to yourself.

If you could count one number per second, it would take you eleven-and-a-half, twenty-four-hour days to reach one million.

If you continue counting, in about thirty-two years you will reach one billion. At one number per second, reaching one trillion will take you almost 32,000 years.

Isn't it odd that we throw these numbers around like we understand them, when in fact we cannot even count that high? To understand demography you need to understand numbers. There are over 6.5 billion people in the world. China and India both have over one billion each. A billion people are a lot of people, but don't try to count them.

Follow the Money: A Transfer of Wealth and Power

The GI Generation saved money, perhaps because of the scare put into them by the Great Depression. *Today, less than five million people are still alive from that generation. They represent a hardy 7 percent of the original seventy million.*

This hardy remainder of the GI Generation, and the Silent Generation after it, holds the bulk of the nation's personal wealth. During the time those five million survivors of the GI Generation have left here on earth, the remainder of almost $10 trillion will pass from one generation to another. Boomers will get most of it. They may also assume positions of power on corporate board seats vacated by their mothers, fathers, and rich relatives.

For a perspective of just how much money we're talking about, compare the trillions of dollars that the Boomers will inherit with the $15 trillion value of the entire U.S. stock market. This transfer of wealth is more than the $6.5 to $7 trillion in annual consumer spending in the United States.

Marketers should be focusing on Boomer spending and the money we'll have to match our mass and motivation. Boomers will spend money on things their parents and grandparents would consider foolish. We'll buy huge houses, expensive boats, trips to Europe, and cruises. Cruise ships can't be built fast enough to accommodate the demand. Boomers might even pay off part of the trillion-dollar U.S. credit card debt. A few of us will actually save or invest this transfer of wealth. But most of us will spend it.

Remember the Golden Rule: He who has the gold rules. Boomers will rule—once the largest transfer of wealth in the history of the world is complete and we inherit the remainder of our parents' $7 to $10 trillion. Corruption in high places will be rampant because of the Boomers' situational-ethics standards.

But mass, money, motivation—and power—will have its upside. The glass ceiling will disappear. Ethnic prejudices will fade. Boomers are very comfortable letting women and minorities have positions of authority. Marijuana will be legal (old habits die hard).

Boomers will refuse to grow old. We will seek, and be able to afford, any product or service that keeps us young, healthy, and vital. We will not buy "old people" services for a long time, if ever (do you know any Boomers with dentures?). We will dote on our Generation Y children and grandchildren. Already, we cannot seem to spend enough on them and we're creating a generation of consumers far surpassing any before it.

Massive opportunity for a marketer's profit is on its way.

> *"There may be a lot of poor old people around in twenty years, but for now, we're seeing the greatest transfer of wealth in the history of the world."*

CHAPTER 8

What Boomers Will Buy

In 2008, the Boomers were forty-four to sixty-three years old. To understand these Boomer consumers, you need to understand that the Boomers will never fit the established historical pattern of this age demographic. The Boomer needs to change things. Even the Boomer funerals will be different—very different.

According to the Bureau of Labor Statistics, consumer spending does a nosedive after fifty (see Figure 8.1).

This makes sense because when you think about it, how much stuff do we really need that we haven't already bought by

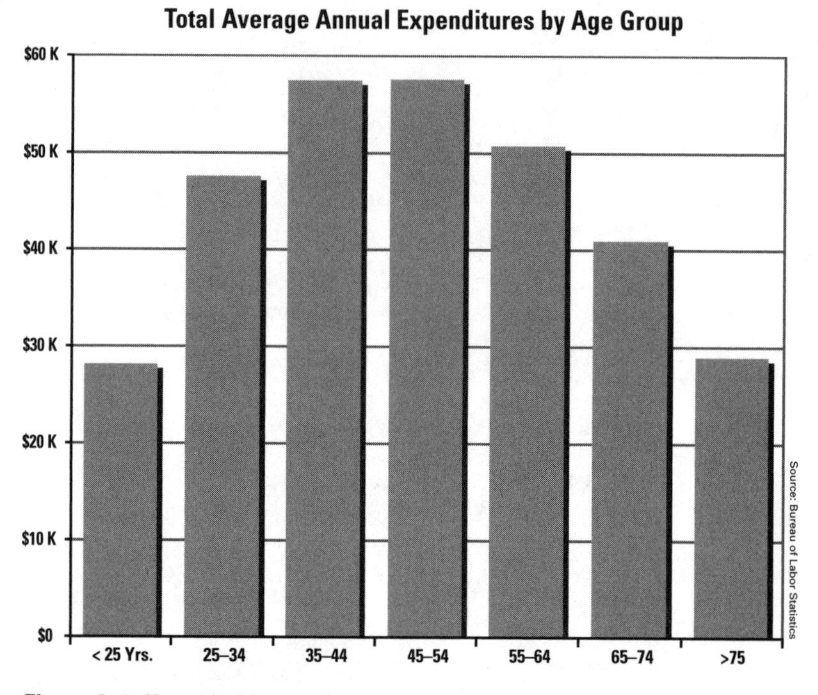

Figure 8–1. *Household spending decreases after age 50.*

age fifty? The issue then becomes what do we do with all the stuff we have amassed? Boomers are not likely to throw things away, especially men. I am convinced that this fact has precipitated the boom in mini-storage facilities—a safe place for stuff.

So if spending goes south after fifty, where *will* Boomers spend their remaining dollars? In general terms, they will spend on recreation, food, health care, convenience, entertainment, transportation, and their grandkids. In any case, to do business with a Boomer, you need to remember the three-prong rule:

1. Make my life easy.

2. Save me some time.

3. Don't rip me off.

That's why the bloom is already off the rose for Harley-Davidson Motorcycles—the market is flooded with used bikes. However, I believe you will see a sharp spike in two-seater cars that empty nesters can finally enjoy. Really good prepared foods from supermarkets and good-value restaurants that don't skimp on portions will do well. Motor homes that get good gas mileage and are very easy to maintain and use will be a huge market.

Big-screen TVs and home-entertainment centers will continue to dominate Boomer buying. It is interesting to note here that technology is moving so quickly that the home-theater experience will always need updating. Boomers can't stand to be behind the times or have old technology that might date them.

Boomers will continue to inhale health care, especially pharmaceuticals—anything that will make them look or feel younger and maybe help them lose weight or keep their hair. (Remember Boomers had a lot of experience with pharmaceuticals in the sixties and seventies.) Natural remedies and holistic medicine will remain strong. Cosmetic surgery will remain very high on the Boomers' lists. A weight-loss pill that really works will sell better than Viagra.

Don't look for Boomers to start using mass transit suddenly when they turn sixty in overwhelming numbers. They are far too independent for that. Boomers will be buying fewer cars, however, because their need to drive kids everywhere will be a memory at that age. SUVs will soon be history. Boomers will look for lower, easy-access, medium-size cars that get reasonable gas mileage. One car that comes to mind is the mid-size Ford Five Hundred. It is easy to get in and out of and has what they call Command Seating. This means Boomers will be able to see other cars because the seats are high and upright.

Boomers are generous. They really spoiled their kids and will continue to do so by helping them buy houses and then helping them fill these houses with stuff. This should provide a respite for the hapless furniture industry. However, the real story about Boomers' generosity will come out when Boomers begin to spoil their grandkids. Trust me, money will be no object and the toy industry will flourish once again. It's called "the bubby factor," *bubby* being an affectionate colloquial name for grandmother. Beware of the coming bubby factor! Think expensive toys.

CHAPTER 9

Boomers Will Not Get Old

As I mentioned in Chapter 6, it was nearly ten years ago that I attempted to convince Horace Deets, who at the time was executive director of AARP, that the AARP was misleading the American public into thinking that the country was going to be overrun with elderly people for decades to come because the Baby Boomers were aging. This perception was certainly to AARP's advantage and gave it enormous power to lobby (and get paid for it), but the fact is it is just dead wrong. AARP's precipitous decline in membership over the past ten years should have been a clue.

Boomers Will Not "Give In"

Remember when Boomers burned their draft cards? I ceremoniously burned my AARP card in front my shocked employees as a measure of my protest. I am not and I never will be my parents. My parents gave in to "old age" in a way that leaves me cold. I guess it's a Boomer thing. I recently had my sixtieth birthday, and someone reminded me that sixty is the new forty. I like that kind of math.

I remember when my mother remarried. It wasn't a happy time for me. I didn't like my stepfather because I knew he really didn't like me. Unfortunately for him, I was part of the package. Kids know. I think we both tried to get along but we both knew we were from different planets. Besides he was old—really old. He was sixty; I was twelve. My mother was forty-four.

It is funny how perceptions shift. My parents' culture and the emerging Boomer culture that I was a part of were light-years apart. Everything about them was different from me. We lived in different worlds. Their clothes, music, cars, art, recreation, ethics, vision, morality, and politics were contrary to my positions and we clashed all the time. Today I am sixty and my youngest daughter is thirteen. We are definitely not the same sixty and thirteen that I knew when I was thirteen. My thirteen-year-old daughter actually thinks I am cool; so does my sixteen-year-old. I work hard at this perception. Boomers, overall, work hard at this perception. My parents were not cool.

People tell me I have a good memory because I can recall details from a very long time ago. I remember everything my stepfather did when he was sixty, and I bear no resemblance to him. He really was an old man. I really am not. I don't think it is just me. I am convinced that Boomers simply are not going to get old the way our parents got old. We won't do it. We refuse. In this way we Boomers have changed the way people are aging.

I will tell you this: I am not going to finish up my time here on earth lying in a bed in an assisted-living facility while some minimum-wage staffer steals my stuff and mixes up my medication. No, I am not going out that way. How will I finish up my time on earth? I don't know. Maybe the Eskimos have it right. When they outlive their usefulness and their ability to contribute, they quietly wander out onto the ice and let the polar bears eat them.

Cashing in on the Boomer Consumers

Marketers who want to capitalize on the aging Boomer consumer will have to be innovative and creative. The simple answer here is to look at the historic products and services that meet the needs and demands of people in their fifties and sixties and make them cool—yes, cool. Remember, Boomers will forever see themselves as hip and cool. That's where the word *hippie* came from.

Did you ever wonder what happened to the millions of hippies? They cut their hair, got married, and blended into society. Secretly, however, they are still hippies at heart.

(Don't believe me? Wait until marijuana is legal. The former hippies will come out of the woodwork to try a little taste of weed again.)

An excellent example of rethinking a product and making it cool is the over-fifty-five community. We can't seem to build them fast enough. Boomers love them. The typical over-fifty-five community is a cool neighborhood of small, one-level, very low-maintenance homes that generally do not allow children to be in residence. There is usually a pool, clubhouse, and maybe even a small golf course. You can have a garden, but the lawns are tiny. Maintenance is minimal and the purchase prices are reasonable. It fits the Boomer criteria: *Make my life easy. Save me some time. Don't rip me off.*

The GI Generation predecessor to the over-fifty-five community was the trailer park. Trailer parks always seem to get hit by tornados. You see this on the news. (Maybe it's God's way of telling us we shouldn't live in trailer parks.) My paternal grandparents lived in a trailer park in Florida. My mother lived in a trailer park in California. I almost fired an employee once for using the phrase "trailer trash." The metaphor speaks volumes.

Boomers would never live in trailer parks. It's not cool. Boomers will continue to gravitate to the over-fifty-five communities in droves. The exception, of course, will be the Boomers who can't sell their 6,000-square-foot starter castles because there aren't enough status-conscious Gen Xers to buy them. The idea of empty nesters living in 6,000 square feet of living space doesn't make a lot of sense, does it? That's not cool.

People often ask me if Boomers will retire to Florida. The answer is: Of course! What's not to like about Florida? They will just be a little slower to go. Remember, seventy-year-old Boomers will act younger and for the most part be healthier than their Silent Generation and GI Generation counterparts.

CHAPTER 10

The Boomer Economy
Of Credit Cards and Gift Cards

Boomers are inheriting an enormous amount of money, and they are going to spend that money into their old age. Unfortunately, Boomers are already spending too much money—creating a precarious mountain of credit card and mortgage debt.

The Insanity of Credit Card Spending

Credit card debt is evidence of terminal math deprivation. I recently paid off all our credit cards after I refinanced my house and was dumbstruck when I discovered that one lender was charging us 28 percent interest. Is there anyone in the world making that kind of return with the possible exception of a loan shark? The only thing that credit card companies don't do is break your knees when your payment is late.

"*Credit cards precipitate legalized criminal behavior. Consumers spend money they do not have and possibly can never pay back. The lenders charge rates that escalate with the consumer's inability to pay.*"

What exactly does 28 percent interest mean? In simple terms let's say you borrow $1,000 from a bank. The interest rate is set at 28 percent *a year* (conventional loan interest calculations are based on one year). If you make *no* payments during that year, your interest will be a whopping $280. Not bad for doing nothing. Also, the people who can least afford it pay the most. No wonder banks love credit cards. Charge!

Credit cards precipitate legalized criminal behavior. Consumers spend money they do not have and possibly can never pay back. (I think this used to be called "stealing.") The lenders charge rates that escalate with the consumer's inability to pay. (I think this was called "usury," or was that "slavery?").

You may not be aware that as a consumer you can call the credit card companies and demand they lower your rate. In most cases, they will do so rather than lose a cash cow. This has spawned a whole new industry of debt counselors who will call the credit card companies for you, get your interest rate lowered, and then charge you a fee. (As I said, you can do this yourself and save the cost of the middleman.)

Keep in mind also that credit card debt is unsecured debt. If you declare bankruptcy, the credit card company gets *nothing*. It is therefore in the company's best interest to keep you financially alive just enough to make the minimum payments—similar to how the slave masters would feed slaves just enough to keep them working. Credit card debt accounts for one-third of the nation's $6.5 trillion in consumer spending. Americans currently have about $1 trillion in credit card debt. (Remember how I told you it would take 32,000 years to count to a trillion?)

That's a frightening thought when you consider that Boomers are responsible for most credit card and consumer spending. They're also spending money from the refinancing of their homes plus what they inherit from their GI Generation parents. If this alarms you, it should. We've built the proverbial house of (credit) cards.

The Insanity of Gift Cards

There is no easier place for math to get away from us then when it has to do with money. I was looking for my sunglasses case one summer day a few months back. In my house, sunglasses cases tend to find their way into top drawers, either in the bedroom, living room, pantry, or kitchen. You see, when sunglasses are left out on a table it bothers my wife because they are in the way. (Of what I don't know, but they are in the way.) She puts them in top drawers. Our top drawers remind me of the flotsam and jetsam that wash up on the riverbank next to our house. You never know what you are going to find, but there are some regular items, like sunglasses cases.

By the time I reached the bedroom, I was getting a little cranky because I wanted my glasses and I had to leave. There they were in the last top drawer left. Next to my case was what appeared to be a stack of credit cards with a rubber band around them. What was this? I couldn't resist. I took the rubber band off and discovered that these were gift cards to retail stores. Some I remember buying for my kids at Christmas, others we probably received as gifts. It's a Boomer thing. Boomers like to give gift cards because it is easy to do and Boomers are basically lazy. Generation Y is often the recipient of the gift card because with their Boomer parents' rate of divorce they are getting gifts from four parents and eight grandparents. It is sort of a good deal. When I was a kid, a gift was a new shirt. To my daughters, a gift is a piece of plastic.

Back to my handful of gift cards. I wondered if there was still money left on them. When I told my wife about the cards later that day, she said, "I was wondering where those were." We found out later that there were still a couple hundred dollars total on the cards. That bothered me. We would not leave a wad of cash in the top drawer. Why would we leave the gift cards there? Because we do not see them as cash, even though for all practical purposes they are the same as cash.

I can remember hanging on to a bunch of American Express travelers' checks until some smart person reminded me that not redeeming the checks was like making an interest-free loan to American Express. We were making an interest-free loan to our favorite retailers by not redeeming the gift cards.

What's even better are the gift cards and certificates that expire. The retailers that do this are saying, "We have borrowed the money from you for so long that now we don't have to pay it back." I believe that there is state and federal legislation that will soon make this illegal. A recent Deloitte & Touche study revealed that the gift card business is now in the hundreds of billions of dollars, and *Consumer Reports* stated that fully *27 percent* of these cards are not redeemed after one year. That means that retailers are getting billions of dollars for free. That's a lot of money. For free.

> *"If you declare bankruptcy, the credit card company gets nothing. It is therefore in the company's best interest to keep you just financially alive enough to make the minimum payments. Credit card debt accounts for one-third of the nation's $6.5 trillion in consumer spending."*

CHAPTER 11

Of Course You Can Afford It!

The housing crisis that seemed to hit "suddenly" in 2007 was actually building for years. It was primarily a Boomer issue precipitated by bad planning, poor borrowing habits, and reckless refinancing—more math-deprived behavior. The Boomer does not understand fiscal responsibility or even how to save money and accumulate wealth. The Boomer understands enjoying life, driving big SUVs, and living in big houses.

Boomers and Car Loans

Volkswagen of America/Porsche/Audi, Inc., in Culver City, California, recruited me out of college. It was a dream job with a lot of perks, including a brand-new car to drive. I had never owned a new car, so when the company gave me the keys to this new Volkswagen Super Beetle, I tried to be cool but there was no way to hide my excitement. I was a kid in a candy store. It had air-conditioning, an AM/FM stereo radio, and a sunroof. And the crème de la crème: the company paid for gas. As part of my corporate training, I was required to sell cars in a Volkswagen dealership for three months. I had just graduated from college, but this is where my real education began.

Volkswagen had a sales formula that was all but written in stone. It was based on strong product knowledge. Volkswagen was proud of its well-made cars. We had to learn all the features of the cars and know them cold. In the sales process, we were to translate the features of the car into real customer benefits and then close the deal by letting the customer decide if this was the right automobile for him or her. It was very noble. We were taught to believe in this process and not deviate from it. We were taught that Detroit's slick-trick methods of selling cars were the antithesis of the Volkswagen Way and were just plain wrong—"dirty" even.

There was a heavy concentration of American automobile dealers in Los Angeles on Figueroa Street. At Volkswagen of America we referred to the salespeople on Figueroa Street as "Figueroa Freddies." This was not a compliment; it was another way of saying "crooked dishonest salesman."

My idealism lasted about two hours at the Volkswagen dealership on Beach Boulevard in Huntington Beach, where I started my actual on-the-job sales training. I was assigned to work with a seasoned professional who would be my mentor for three months. My first tip-off that something was up should have been the fact that my mentor wore sunglasses on the showroom floor. Frank was a colorful guy who knew the ropes and sold a lot of cars, but the ropes he knew bore no resemblance to the Volkswagen Way. We would wait on customers together.

I very quickly learned that there were only three things that mattered: (1) Did we have the car that the customer had already decided on? (2) Did we have the lowest price? (3) Could we get the customer financing if the customer needed it? The car part was easy. We either had it or we didn't. Did we have the lowest price? That was a game we played with other Volkswagen dealers, and you would sometimes lose a sale for fifty dollars. The trick was to get people to shop the other dealers first because it was the last dealer they shopped that nearly always got the deal.

The interesting challenge was the financing. People with good credit would generally provide their own bank financing and show up with bank checks to pick up their cars. The buyers with poor or bad credit were at your mercy. The easiest way to get them a loan was to embellish their earnings, time on the job, and their net worth. Another name for this is "lying." Sure, you could justify representing your client in the best possible light—that's one way of looking at it—but the bottom line was that if you wanted to get a loan for someone with bad credit or no credit, you lied.

It got worse. In order for these car buyers to get the loans that they probably couldn't afford, they had to overpay for them in the form of high interest. Somehow that was ok because the finance companies that made the loans were aware of the risk but were willing to take their chances because of the high returns. The key variable here is the degree of lying or misrepresentation of the borrower's ability to repay. If too much lying goes on, then too many cars are repossessed and the dubious system breaks down.

All anyone really cares about is making money. Everybody overlooks the lying if the number of failed loans is at a manageable level. Sometimes good market conditions, where unemployment is very low, can actually improve the performance of questionable loans, but more often than not any negative influence will expose their real value. In the business, this is called "bad paper." I soon discovered that there is the world we think we live in, and then there is the real world—the dark underbelly.

The Housing Bubble Bursts

Let's fast-forward to the housing market here in the United States because there are some very similar dynamics taking place. In the last ten or fifteen years many of the almost eighty million Baby Boomers (born between 1945 and 1964) built their dream homes. Many built starter castles of 5,000-plus square feet just in time for their kids to leave home, go off to college, and then get married. I am not even going to debate the merits of this concept of shelter; I'll simply say that this was a bad move demographically.

The Boomers know that they can't stay in these houses indefinitely because the upkeep is too expensive to be practical and they simply no longer need the space. In addition, most starter castles are multilevel and Boomers will eventually need simpler one-level floor plans. A lot of these huge houses are on the market, but there are no buyers because Generation X (born between 1965 and 1984) simply does not have the critical mass necessary to provide the demand. *Remember, there are nine million fewer of them than the Boomers.* Assuming that translates into couples, that means there are over four million fewer home buyers than needed. This is a real problem that will not correct demographically for twenty years. Gulp!

Wait, there's more! Unscrupulous lenders in the subprime category further exacerbate this demographic dilemma. A subprime loan is one that is made to an individual with less than sterling credit; that is, a person who is at risk for repaying the loan. Once again people who will probably have trouble repaying a loan are overcharged for the privilege of trying, just like with car financing.

It is also important to note that many of the subprime victims are first- and second-generation immigrants and Latinos. Remember Latinos flooded the entry-level labor market when the diminutive Generation X could not fill the footprint left behind by the Boomers. As long as the housing market was strong, subprime loans were not only tolerated, they were encouraged. Was the integrity of the subprime loans in question? Of course it was. But everyone looked the other way because all anyone really cared about was making money. A predictable problem has precipitated from the subprime mortgage companies lying too much while they buried their victims in no-down-payment, high-interest, variable-rate mortgages. By the way, the rates do not adjust down. They almost always adjust up—way up.

The subprime mortgage companies made a lot of money. So did attorneys, title insurance companies (who often pay attorneys a 60 percent commission on the premium of the title insurance), appraisers, and financial institutions. Loans were typically bundled and resold to huge publicly traded financial conglomerates who wanted to get in on this high-return, high-risk scheme. But then the bubble burst. The people who couldn't afford mortgages in the first place did something very predictable. They didn't pay their mortgages. This, of course, led to an avalanche of foreclosures and billions in write-offs by respected financial institutions. This all sent Wall Street reeling.

Will we recover from this debacle? As a nation, we always do. But there are also several underlying demographic reasons to assume that the housing market will straighten itself out.

- Generation Y, now twenty-three and under, will buy homes much earlier than its Boomer parents because included in its number is a very large, very young, high-paid contingent of trained technicians and an enormous number of budding entrepreneurs.

- Women are becoming home buyers. As the conservative (and perhaps somewhat misogynistic) GI Generation finally vacates its remaining board seats, the glass ceiling will shatter and women will be welcomed to C-level positions in major corporations and elsewhere. Aspiring independent women will be the newcomers to the housing market for the upscale homes. Pity the real estate agent who insists that a buyer's husband be part of the decision-making process.

  (I recently told a friend that women could easily hold 60 percent of the nation's top management jobs within the next ten years. He looked at me pensively and said, "I hope they treat us better than we treated them." It's true. Women could treat men very poorly in the workplace for a very long time before they ever evened the score.)

- Management's "perfect storm"—the shortage of midlevel managers—will avail unprecedented opportunity to minorities and immigrants to advance their careers. Latinos and African Americans will find that commonplace racial barriers to corporate advancement will no longer exist. Along with advancement comes more money and bigger salaries. This will easily put home ownership within reach. A new market? Big time!

- Finally, this new housing market does not flow from a positive trend. Crime in the United States is spiking and will continue to do so for another decade. High-risk young men in the crime-committing age will be unemployed in record numbers. These young men will tend to congregate in cities. As a result, the relative tranquility that cities have enjoyed for the last twenty years will be breached. Cities will not be safe and people who have opted to live in cities over the last twenty years will probably not want to live there anymore. They will move out and buy homes away from the cities, especially if they have kids. This is not good for the economies of the cities, but it will be a shot in the arm for the housing market elsewhere.

CHAPTER 12

Social Security and Private Health Care

Dead But Not Buried

Social Security and our private health care system, financed by health insurance, have a great deal in common. Both involve a flow of money going in and a flow of money going out. As long as the flow of money going in exceeds the flow of money going out plus the expenses of operating the system, things are good. Both Social Security and our private health care system depend on large young generations to provide the money that flows in so the money flowing out meets the needs of older generations. *In the United States we have a diminutive Generation X following a huge aging Boomer Generation. In other words, we have a problem—a big problem.*

Social Security Is a Ponzi Scheme

Even people who can't count know that Social Security won't feed the Boomers. Boomers have not allowed for their own retirement by saving as their parents did. Instead, they have lived off of their parents' savings, which they will continue to inherit.

But what happens when that's gone? The last of the Boomers' parents, those eighty-five-plus-year-olds of the GI Generation, are dying. There are about five million of them left out of a group of about sixty million born between 1905 and 1924.

This last five million is a hardy bunch, living well past the average age when we are supposed to die (seventy-two for men, seventy-six for women). Why are they so resilient? It might have something to do with the fact that people who are well-to-do can afford good health care, and good health care has a lot to do with living longer.

This remaining five million people still control *much of* the nation's personal wealth and board seats. That makes them very powerful and influential, but not for much longer. They will die, and the Boomers will inherit what remains of the $7 to $10 trillion dollars, a figure representing the GI Generation's total personal wealth. Boomers will mark the receipt of their inheritance by buying starter castles and large boats. Others will pay off some of the trillion dollars of credit card debt. In short, the Boomers are blowing through this money.

But many others will invest in the stock market. So look for a spike in the values of many securities, especially high-risk investments, because Boomers have to make up for lost time. After all, the best customer for the stock market is a male in his late forties (remember the Boomer peak birth year was 1957). Most Boomers will wish their parents had saved more, and they will be forced to turn to a frail Social Security for a scary retirement, featuring a very low fixed income.

It gets worse. Social Security cannot possibly survive. It's really a Ponzi scheme that succeeds only when more people pay in than are being paid. Right now we have the equivalent of eight people paying in and three collecting. Under this scenario, the system is just making it.

But when Boomers start collecting as a group, the system will go bankrupt—if in fact Social Security makes it that far. According to a June 2004 study by the United States Congressional Budget Office, titled "The Outlook for Social Security," Social Security outlays will exceed revenues starting in 2019 and not reverse for the foreseeable future.

In a *San Francisco Chronicle* interview (February 13, 2005), former Congressional Budget Office Director Douglas Holtz-Eakin, a high-level Bush administration economist, was asked about the problem.

> **Q:** What is the size of Social Security's financial problem?
>
> **A:** The benefits promised in Social Security rise above the revenues dedicated to Social Security and stay above as far as the eye can see.

We could have a bigger elderly homeless population, which is an ugly thought. But then I never said this would be pretty.

> *"Look for a spike in the values of many securities, especially high-risk investments, because Boomers have to make up for lost time . . . . Most will wish their parents had saved more, and they will be forced to turn to a frail Social Security for a scary retirement, featuring a very low fixed income."*

Socialized Medicine—a Boomer Mandate

The insurance business is a business. Businesses must make a profit or they won't remain businesses very long. The operative word here is *profit.* And profit is not a four-letter word. It is the essential ingredient in any business.

Let's examine how the health insurance business makes a profit. I pay $18,000 a year for medical insurance for my family of four. My wife and I calculated that if we had to pay cash for our covered medical needs, the tab would be about $7,500. So on balance the health insurance company made a gross profit of $10,500 on our account.

All things being equal, we are probably good customers but not as good as we once were. There have been years when we paid in, and with the exception of routine physicals, we had no claims.

Insurance companies need lots of customers who pay in and make no claims. Why? Because that is the only way they can offer insurance protection to people who do make lots of claims. The principle is shared risk.

So in a nutshell, a profitable health insurance company is one that has more customers paying in who do not make claims than people paying in who do make them.

Sound simple? It is. But believe me, it's not well understood. Here is where understanding generational demography comes into play. At certain ages in life, our likelihood of needing health care is much greater than at other ages. Most pregnancies occur between the age of twenty-five and thirty-five. They are expensive propositions. The cost of a complicated pregnancy and a premature birth can reach the high five figures within a nanosecond.

Next to premature births, the biggest medical expense is dying. Most of us will spend more on health care in the last seventy-two hours of our lives than we spend in our entire lifetime. Intensive care has an equally intensive price tag.

So who is dying? You guessed it: the Boomers. Take a look at the U.S. birth chart in chapter 1 again. Boomers overwhelm the chart. In 2008, they were in a very unprofitable age range for medical insurers—the age range where people have heart attacks, get cancer, and become very reliant on medication.

Trust me, there are *not* a lot of Boomers paying for health insurance and not making claims. The Boomers love medication. They had a lot of practice self-medicating in the '60s and '70s.

A simple analysis of your local obituary page over the course of a couple of months will show you that there are almost as many people age forty-four to sixty-three dying than people between sixty-four and eighty-three. How can this be? Doesn't this defy logic?

> *"Most of us will spend more on health care in the last seventy-two hours of our lives than we spend in our entire lifetime. Intensive care has an equally intensive price tag. So who is dying? You guessed it: the Boomers."*

No. It would only be illogical only if the two groups were the same size, which they aren't, as I've told you again and again. *There were almost eighty million Boomers born from 1945 to 1964 and 52.5 million Silents born from 1925 to 1944.* The only people outdying the Boomers are the people over eighty. In just a few years, when the GI Generation is gone, the Boomers will assume the "dying and infirm" title and hold it for the next thirty years. So who will compensate for what the Boomers are not paying into the health insurance kitty? You won't like the answer: No one and eventually everyone.

The only answer to the enormous health care crisis in the United States is socialized medicine. We need health care. It must be paid for. A normal, share-the-risk health insurance model cannot work. Period.

About ten years ago I counseled a high-level executive at Aetna regarding the company's impending purchase of U.S. Healthcare. I remember saying, "Don't do it." He looked at me incredulously and said, "Why not? U.S. Healthcare was a cash cow for years and their management ruined it. Aetna's management team is far superior. We'll fix it and make a fortune." Aetna bought U.S. Healthcare and proceeded to dump a lot of time, effort, and money into the company before admitting that a fix was not forthcoming. It is the demography, not the company or the management, that is calling the plays in shared-risk health care.

Our existing health care system is in shambles. It doesn't work for anyone. The doctors can't make ends meet. The insurers can't make ends meet. The insured aren't getting fair value for their premiums. The cost of health insurance in the United States increased a whopping 6.1 percent in 2007, more than the increases in an average worker's wages (3.7 percent) and the inflation rate (2.6 percent), according to a September 2007 Kaiser Family Foundation report. Workers now pay an average of $3,281 a year to cover their share of a family policy, according to the study. Employers paid over $12,000 for a family premium in 2007, a whopping 78 percent increase since 2001, according to the Kaiser report. Ouch!

Before you start with sweeping indictments and finger-pointing at the hated attorneys and their abuse of medical malpractice claims, or at the greedy insurers, or at the self-ish doctors, or all those insured hypochondriacs, stop. Those issues are only symptoms of the real problem. The three component players in our health care system are behaving not unlike the internal departments of any large business that's going under. When money is in short supply, life becomes a game of musical chairs. The love is gone. It's every man for himself.

The bottom line is this: Our health care system must make a profit at multiple levels and it can't. It can't, because of unfavorable demography, and there is nothing you can do to change that simple fact. Do the math.

> *"So who will compensate for what the Boomers are not paying into the health insurance kitty? You won't like the answer: No one and eventually everyone."*

CHAPTER 13

Wal-Mart Hits a Wall—A Great Wall

Wal-Mart is essentially a Baby Boomer–based business, but I don't get a sense that they are aware of it.

Inside statistics about Wal-Mart customers and demography are hard to come by. You have to respect the company's ability to play its hand so close to the vest despite its size. However, in an October 2006 Wal-Mart.com webcast, two top Wal-Mart.com executives gave a rare but very revealing glimpse of who they say is Wal-Mart's best customer. A story on the webcast appeared on WashingtonPost.com on October 24, 2006, and was written by Frank Ahrens.

According to the story, Chief Executive Officer Carter Cast and Chief Marketing Officer Raul Vazquez took turns answering questions. Ahrens wrote that Vazquez was animated; Cast, not so much. Cast did say, however, that research helped Wal-Mart create a composite picture of its best customer: She is a woman in her early forties, lives in the suburbs, and has "several" children. "We call her Nancy," Cast said. If Nancy is a real profile resulting from research, then Wal-Mart has a problem. Nancy, Wal-Mart's best customer, is a stationary demographic positioned perfectly and directly in front of the advancing Grand Canyon of Generation X. If Wal-Mart expects Generation X to buy quantities of stuff at the same level as the Baby Boom Generation, which has aged out of Wal-Mart's best customer demographic, it's as dumb as a stump and can't count.

Note that in 2007 Raul Vazquez became president and CEO of Wal-Mart Stores Inc.'s Walmart.com. Carter Cast is now leading the parent company's U.S. business strategy and strategic planning. I wonder if he took "Nancy" with him.

Wal-Mart's lack of foresight is starting to surface in recent figures showing flat same-store sales. Because Wal-Mart has routinely enjoyed double-digit same-store sales increases for decades, these figures are a real cause for concern. In Wal-Mart's 2007 annual report, President and CEO Lee Scott stated that he was disappointed with the overall same-store 2 percent increases because they fell well short of Wal-Mart's plan.

The lackluster sales precipitated management's usual knee-jerk reactions when it has no idea why sales are off. What did the famous retailer do? It cleaned house in the marketing department, brought in a top-level marketing executive from Chrysler, fired its advertising agency, and charted a new marketing/merchandising course into higher-end merchandise and fashion. Well, it is no surprise that all of this has already failed to produce any glimpse of a turnaround, and the high-end idea has already been abandoned. Big does not always mean smart. In this case, big is stupid. Take a breath, Wal-Mart, and consider the following.

Wal-Mart's retail concept is narrow, cheap, and deep. This means its success is built on low price, limited selection, and vast quantities (of merchandise generally made in China). Remember, the more of one thing people produce or buy, generally the cheaper it gets. To its credit, Wal-Mart is almost never out of product and does have very low prices. By comparison, Target has a much broader selection but higher prices.

Where Wal-Mart is going to get tripped up is on selection. You see, Wal-Mart has figured out what the mature Boomer market buys. It has refined this demand to the narrowest selection possible, almost telling Boomers what they will buy. Boomers, in turn, are ok with this because when you are between forty and sixty years old, you have rather defined tastes and preferences that influence your purchasing habits. In this case, if Wal-Mart does not have what Boomers really want but does have something close at a very low price, Boomers will buy it.

So where is the rub? Simple. When a consumer hits about fifty years old, his or her demand for purchases begins to subside. At sixty years old, you pretty much have all the stuff you need and then some. Your body has stopped changing, so you can wear clothes longer—a lot longer. If you want to see what was fashionable thirty years ago, go to a Miami retirement community. The point here is that the bloom is off the rose of Boomer consumption. The Boomer population is a huge bell-shaped curve, with the leading edge turning sixty-three. The peak of the curve turned fifty in 2007.

All of this means that Wal-Mart needs to find a new market fast if it wants to continue doing business. But where does it turn? The two U.S. generations over sixty do not have the critical mass to serve its infrastructure. The U.S. population between twenty-four and forty-three years old (which now numbers eighty million) is a nonhomogeneous combination of the undersized, native-born Generation X and the free-standing market of Latino immigrants. The Latino market is not geographically diverse. Latinos have settled in pockets and have high concentrations in certain states like California, Arizona, Texas, Illinois, Florida, Connecticut, and New York. In states where the Latino population is low, Wal-Mart is going to have to go looking for "Nancy" among the diminutive Generation X. Good Luck.

So who's left? Generation Y, born between 1985 and 2010. *Generation Y will be the largest and most powerful group of consumers this nation has ever seen.* Its members are already consuming at 500 percent of their parents' level in adjusted dollars age for age.

Will Generation Y be the solution to Wal-Mart's sales problems? No. Generation Y is a fickle emerging market, a huge bell-shaped curve with its peak only eighteen years old. They are inhaling entertainment products, fashion, food, electronics, and transportation. Selection is everything to them. They do not care about low price unless it's exactly the item they want. Their tastes change daily. They don't know what they will want six months from now. Wal-Mart's limited-selection, low-price offering to the Boomer will not and can not translate to this group. In short, there is no new market for Wal-Mart unless it dramatically changes who it is—and it probably is too big and entrenched to make this change in time.

Wal-Mart is the world's largest retailer. I shop there. There simply is no other store that sells automotive maintenance products for less. However, I don't feel good in Wal-Mart. My shopping experience is not unpleasant, but it is not pleasant. It is kind of empty. A Wal-Mart store is not a happy place, no matter how many of their unhappy employees tell you to "Have a nice day." This is a store without a soul. Its success has come on the backs of too many people, and this is a fact Wal-Mart feels no need to hide. It has wiped out thousands of small businesses across America and elsewhere. It is ruthless and brutal to its suppliers and employees. It seems to be striving to develop a business model where everyone does the work except the people who get the real money.

It is fitting that Wal-Mart is so tight with China. China is a country with no soul and no moral compass. China's abuse of its own labor force at the behest of its best customer, Wal-Mart, is an injustice whose consequence will come home to roost in due time.

I have been writing about Wal-Mart on my blog. It is no surprise to me that these journal entries are often visited by Chinese who are probably a little antsy about Wal-Mart's lackluster performance of late. I am sure that Wal-Mart is squeezing its Chinese suppliers for better deals to make up for its own shortcomings. The Chinese are sure to retaliate with shoddy products whenever they can. It bears watching. (You can eat Chinese food, but don't eat food from China.)

Incidentally, China's thirty-year-old one-child policy, which has precipitated three decades of male children, is a demographic disaster of epic proportions. The Chinese didn't shoot themselves in the foot, they blew their foot right off! They have wrecked their future workforce. I have not studied the ramifications, but I don't see how China can ever recover from such a calamity. Estimates range from 80 million to 400 million as the number of pregnancies prevented by China's one-child policy. You simply cannot tamper with natural reproduction on such a massive scale and not reap devastating results.

It's true that China has a huge population, over 1.3 billion, but as a result of the one-child policy it is now disproportionate. Ask yourself: Who will feed the old people in forty years? My guess? When the elderly Chinese are no longer productive, they will "disappear" much the same way girl babies have. As this tiny generation of men enters the Chinese labor force, it will not do so for slave wages. This will affect the Chinese economy and send it into a tailspin all by itself. And what is going to happen when all these Chinese men discover that there aren't enough women to marry? That will make them cranky, don't you think? China will be known as the nation without wives. When you don't have wives, you don't have babies. When you don't have babies, you are all done.

CHAPTER 14

Media's Slow Death

The End of Marketing As We Know It

I was watching the six o'clock news, surfing with my remote control among CBS, ABC, and NBC. Watching television and channel surfing is a very Boomer thing. Boomers and television grew up at the same time. We are joined at the hip. The news is important to me because, after all, it is The Fourth Estate. The name was coined long ago in England, signifying that the press was an important fourth part of government representing the people. The press keeps government honest. It is one more element in our wonderful system of checks and balances here in the United States.

So off I went in search of the news. Sometimes you can catch a story on one network while the others are airing commercials, but not always. It seems that the networks have an agreement to air their commercial spots at exactly the same time. It forces people like me to watch commercials, which is really my part of the deal. The networks provide us with valuable information and entertainment in exchange for our attention to their commercial messages. It is the system and it has worked for generations, until now.

You see, the TV networks have upped the ante. When I had an ad agency ten years ago, we would scream if there were more than eight thirty-second commercial spots in a half-hour news show. We would argue that our clients' messages would get lost and that the dominance of commercials would erode the viewers' interest. Today there are three major breaks in the evening news with at least eight commercials or promos each. That's a 300 percent increase in what we are paying with our attention to receive the news.

Hold on, there is more! While I was surfing with my remote I noticed that when I did catch a glimpse of a news story, the quality of the reporting was very shallow and very brief. The stories are nothing more than sound bites. In essence, the networks have increased the cost of the news by 300 percent and reduced the volume and value of the news by at least two-thirds. Ad agencies must continue to buy airtime only because they have no choice and the ads still work to some extent. That's the only reason I can think of.

The remnants of the GI Generation, the tiny Silent Generation, and the Baby Boomers still watch a lot of commercial TV, but even their viewing time is falling off or being fragmented. According to Journalism.org's study, titled "The State of the Media 2006, an Annual Report on American Journalism," the three major news networks (ABC, NBC, and CBS) have lost over twenty-five million viewers combined between 1980 and 2005—a precipitous drop of nearly 50 percent! My point here is that this form of news reporting that is so important to our system will eventually go away forever. Radio news is already history, and newspapers are dead but haven't fallen over yet.

According to the same report from www.Journalism.org, United States weekday newspaper circulation dropped by nearly 13 percent, from about sixty-three million in 1990 to about fifty-five million in 2004. Check for yourself. If your newspaper is full of wire-service stories and has no classified ads to speak of, its reporters are gone and so is its readership.

Generation X and Generation Y do not get their information and entertainment through conventional media, so its commercial future is not uncertain, it's over. This is the end of an era. More importantly it's the end of The Fourth Estate as we know it.

But the question of who will keep government honest is not the only issue raised by the death of mass media. Marketing plays a strategic role in moving goods and services—and marketing is nothing without media vehicles to tell the story.

There is a rule in marketing and advertising: "Go fishing where the fish are." What this means simply is that your greatest efficiencies or return on investment (ROI) are found in media expenditures that deliver the greatest number of bodies (listeners, viewers, readers, or drivers) in your customer demo. So if your customer is a male who is twenty to sixty years old and you sell your product nationally, a 2008 Super Bowl TV buy could make a lot of sense for you. Thirty-second Super Bowl spots sold on average for $2.7 million and delivered 100 million viewers—about one-third of the U.S. population and about 70 percent of its men.

The problem is, apart from the Super Bowl, there are few television shows that can deliver such astounding numbers of viewers. Advertisers and marketers devote significant money as a percentage of their revenues to stimulate sales. For example, supermarkets designate only about one percent of their gross sales to promotion because the gross margin in food is small; apparel and footwear is about 3 percent; automotive about 6 percent; and furniture about 10 to 12 percent. The amounts vary and grow as gross margin increases. Mass media is, undeniably, an important part of commerce in the United States. Some estimates put total advertising and marketing spending at close to $600 billion, with about $300 to $400 billion going to media. As audiences shift from conventional media to fragmented online sources for their information and entertainment, marketers are scrambling to figure out "where the fish are."

In the end, we will not only find it difficult to keep government honest, but without a solid mass media base it is going to be a challenge to sell our products and services.

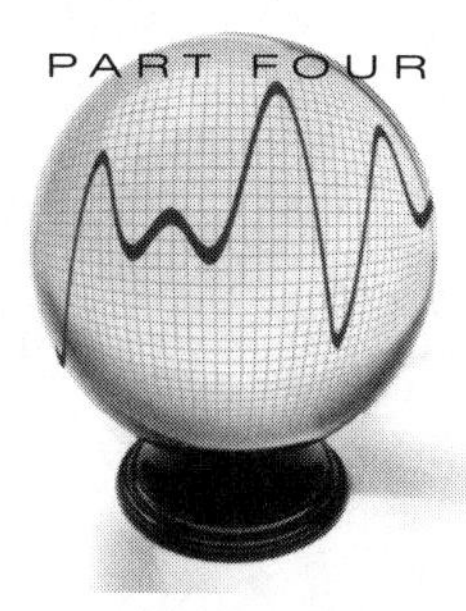

Generation X

The Outsize Expectations of a Small Generation

CHAPTER 15

Quit Picking on the Xers!

What would you think hearing someone criticize a group of 500 people for their poor turnout at the polls compared to another group of a thousand? What if this critic also found fault with this group of 500 for not contributing the same amount of money to their political parties and for not helping out at campaign headquarters like the group of a thousand? You would no doubt see an unreasonable critic with a math problem.

But wait. Don't we do this everyday? We compare groups and draw incorrect conclusions because we do not consider size.

Generation X's Bad Rap

People have mistakenly maligned Generation X for years for not performing "at the level of the Boomers." A prominent book even pointed out the poor performance I just described and portrays Gen Xers as selfish, lazy slackers. The author completely missed the fact that this issue is quantitative, not qualitative.

In fact, Xers contribute money to their parties, turn out at polls, and participate actively in government *at a rate equal to Boomers age for age.* There just aren't as many of them. Between 1945 and 1964 (the Boomer generation) about seventy-eight million babies were born in the United States. *Between 1965 and 1984 (Gen X) there were about sixty-nine million born—or about nine million fewer. That's an 11 percent reduction.*

Are there differences between the rates of political participation of Generation X and the Baby Boomer generation? Yes, there is, but it is more age-related than generation-related. Just drawing from my own experience having handled many political campaigns in my career, the rule of thumb is 80 percent of eligible elderly voters vote and only 20 percent of newly eligible young voters vote. In between these two extremes the rate of participation increases with age. It is sad but true.

When you think about it, it would be easy to develop a dark psychological complex if everyone was always disappointed in you. It starts in the maternity wards across the United States. I heard a story about a radio station in the rural Midwest that sponsored a "First Baby of the Year Contest" in the mid-1970s. It was a tradition whereby the first baby born on January 1 would be lavished with gifts and services. The contest was local, but it was a pretty big deal, and folks would always tune in for the results. The problem was there were no babies born at the local hospitals on January first or the second or the third. It wasn't until the beginning of the next week that they had a winner. This should have been a tip-off to the fact that something was up. But no one noticed and no one questioned this anomaly.

I graduated from an inner-city high school in Middletown, Connecticut, in 1966. I am told that Middletown High School is the oldest public high school in the United States. It started in a nearby library in the 1840s and moved to the existing building in the 1860s when construction was completed. The words *high school* are in stone on the front of the building, as if that was enough description to set it apart from other schools.

Middletown High School remained an active high school in this same building for over 120 years until the birth dearth that is Generation X shut its doors forever. The old building was no longer needed. Middletown kids who had been in two high schools were now consolidated into one. The building was sold and redeployed as elderly housing for the GI Generation. Again, no one gave this anomaly a second thought.

Generation X's "disappointing" performance goes on and on. The United States military had a problem recruiting its members. Fast-food employers couldn't get them to work. They didn't buy enough Levi's jeans. They weren't buying Japanese motorcycles. They weren't buying Detroit's cars. They didn't overwhelm rock concerts or fill bleacher seats at big-league sports events. Now, they are not buying the Boomer's starter castles and very soon they won't be able to carry this nation's tax burden when it becomes their turn. *All this because there are nine million fewer of them than the Baby Boomers.*

Gen Xers have copied the Boomers (there were a lot of "those older kids on the playground"). But Gen Xers deserve a lot of respect for actually attempting to perform at the level of the Boomers. We've been pitting a team of eleven ball players against a team of nine. I'll say it again: *Gen X is 11 percent smaller than the Boomer generation.*

The Truth About Generation X

It's a sad commentary on how we aren't doing the math. But don't be too sad. For every ten jobs the Boomers leave behind, there'll be only nine people to fill them. So Xers will have their pick of the best jobs. Furthermore, 50 percent of Xers are college-educated, compared with 25 percent of the Boomers. And Gen X has the potential for producing a higher percentage of top-caliber professionals. This is a qualitative issue.

Pound for pound, this team of nine could be the better set of players, but it will forever be plagued by its diminutive size compared to the Boomers.

Oddly, many companies will actually benefit by attracting, recruiting, and retaining Generation X employees because the process will be very competitive. Competition is good. Competition makes you sharp. People will credit Generation X with improving the workplace because its members will be able to make demands without fear of reprisal.

Members of Generation X will bring their dogs to work. Generation Xers will definitely not need the help of unions. They will remain 100 percent employed and very much in demand.

Selling products and services to Generation X is a bit of a trick. The only way you can grow a business with Generation X as a primary customer is to have a brand-new product or service. If your product or service has an established infrastructure that was meant to meet the demands of the Boomers, who have since aged out of your market and been replaced by Generation X, you have a problem. However, if you have a new product or service that is targeted at the current Generation X age demo, the fact that they are a small generation following a big one doesn't mean a thing. Generation X is, after all, over sixty-nine million people strong. Some excellent examples of new products embraced by Generation X are the personal computer, the cell phone, the BlackBerry, portable GPS, snowboards, and now the iPod.

We will explore in the marketing implications of the Gen X consumer. But first, let's look at the social causes and implications of this undersize generation in Chapter 16.

> *"Xers contribute money to their parties, turn out at polls, and participate actively in government at a rate equal to the Boomers age for age.* ***There just aren't as many of them."***

CHAPTER 16

The Cause and Effect of a Small Generation

Of all the factors that effect demography, the most important are total birthrate and total fertility rate. The United States is currently the only Western country with a total rate of fertility that is above replacement level. But what is replacement level?

Well, let's assume there are ten couples on a deserted island. If they want to maintain a constant number of people on the island, how many children must each couple have? The answer is two. What if one of the couples proves to be unable to have kids? Then how many kids will the remaining couples have to have to maintain the population? The answer is 2.2. This is the total fertility rate. What if two of the men decide to pair off or two of the women want to be a couple? This complicates fertility.

Why is a constant population important anyway? Wouldn't it be better if there were just fewer people? The rationale sounds logical: less pollution, less crime, fewer mouths to feed, and more space.

The problem is that there is a natural order that must be maintained if a community large or small wants to sustain itself. As described in the next section, there are two short periods in our migration through time when we are dependent: when we are young and when we are old. There is one long period, as adults, when we are not only required to be self-sufficient but we must also do our part to care for the dependents—children and the elderly.

The Stages of Our Lives

When we are born, we are totally reliant on others. We eat a lot and produce nothing. If we were left alone, we would die. We gradually become more and more self-reliant as we age. In theory at least, when we are in our twenties, we begin to make our own way. We can provide for ourselves. What we eat is on par with what we produce. As we age through our thirties, we begin to produce more than we eat, so we provide for others who are producing less than they eat. As we age through our forties, others' dependence on our ability to produce a lot more than we eat becomes very great and peaks when we reach age fifty, when we are at the height of our producing years.

Between fifty and sixty, our production begins to diminish as does others' reliance on us. Between sixty and eighty we tend to be self-reliant, meeting our own needs. After eighty, the total dependence starts all over again. We can no longer effectively produce, but we still eat and require care. This principal of reliance and provision exists in families, cultures, and countries throughout the world and dates back to the beginnings of humankind. It is a natural balance that is so powerful it drives economies and sustains nations.

In terms of generations, the principal of reliance and provision means that each generation must provide for the generation preceding it (now elderly) and the generation that follows it (still children). So what does Generation X have to do with this principal? Due in large part to the reduced fertility in the United States between 1965 and 1984, *Generation X has about nine million fewer people than the Baby Boomer generation it follows and about thirty million fewer people than the Generation Y it precedes.* Generation X is taking over the role of the nation's provider, and it can't possibly succeed—it doesn't have the critical mass.

As a nation we will begin to feel this phenomenon intensify as we try to tax this generation to meet our needs. Federal, state, and local taxes will all suffer—big time.

Generation X and Taxes

As you can see in Figure 16.1, household income peaks for wage earners in their late forties and early fifties. Then it falls off, creating a bell curve. I believe we can safely make the claim that this bell curve could represent the amount of income tax paid by the respective households as well, as income tax paid is tied to the amount of income. In addition, I think we can safely assume that the more money a household makes the more it spends, and that this fact would influence the amount of sales tax paid by these households. Finally, it would be safe to conclude that the biggest and most expensive homes would belong

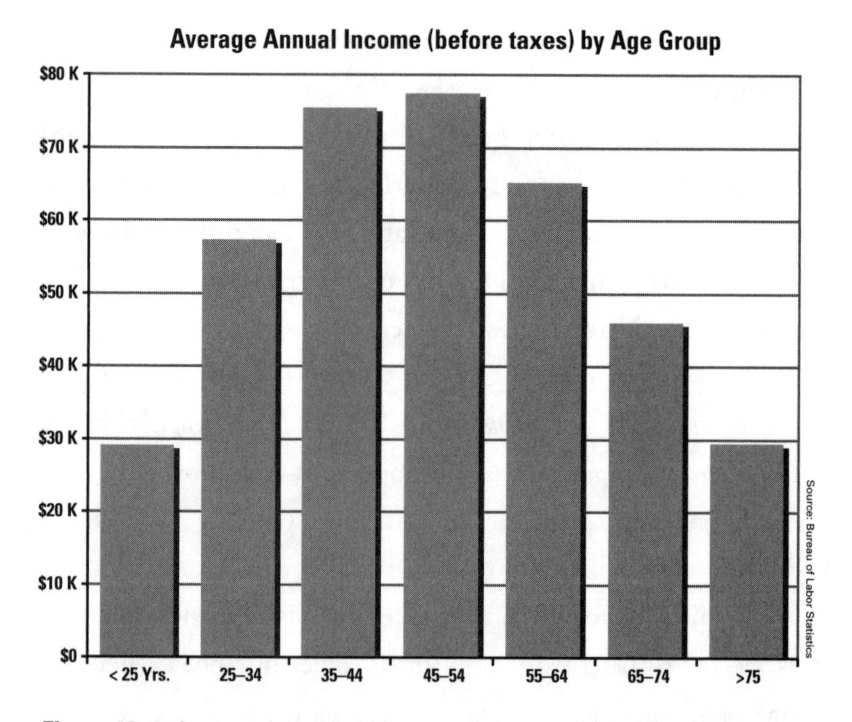

Figure 16–1. *Average household income before taxes, by age, 2004.*

to those who could most likely afford them. So the biggest property tax burden falls to the biggest earners as well.

At this time, the biggest earners are from the Boomer Generation. But as Generation Xers enter the age at which society expects them to carry the tax burden, they won't be able to do it. There are just not enough of them. We could well end up short of enough money to run our federal, state, and local governments.

My question is this: Why don't we hear the presidential candidates discussing this subject? This is far more important and potentially dangerous than anything they are currently debating.

The Effect of Legalized Abortion on Generation X

An argument can be made that *Roe v. Wade*, the 1973 Supreme Court decision that legalized abortion, has had a significant impact on U.S. demography—specifically by reducing the size of Generation X. The statistics are huge and tantalizing.

Since January 22, 1973—the date of the decision—about 45 million legal abortions have been recorded in the United States. According to the Centers for Disease Control and Prevention (CDC), this thirty-one-year period saw approximately 1.5 million abortions performed per year—nearly four thousand per day. Comparing these statistics to four million live births in a robust year, it would appear that we terminate about 27 percent of pregnancies.

In recent years, the U.S. abortion rate has declined slightly to a yearly 1.3 million. Boomer women, even those who dared having their children later in life, have aged beyond their fertile years. But the number of abortions will rebound dramatically when the Gen Y peak becomes more sexually active. A rebound will also occur in sexually transmitted diseases, especially AIDS. Epidemics will replace our present respite, simply owing to a giant, emerging number of young people in the age most vulnerable to getting and spreading them.

It's true that many abortions are drastic birth control rather than population-control measures; in other words, a young woman who had an abortion as a teen may still have four planned kids when she gets married. Still, there can be little doubt that without abortions there would be significantly more Generation Xers, as evidenced by the immediate plunge in fertility rate after the Supreme Court decision. According to the National Center for Health Statistics, the fertility rate of U.S. women dropped from eighty-eight children per 1,000 women age fifteen to forty-four in 1970 to sixty-six children in 1975—a 25 percent fall.

CHAPTER 17

The X Factor
Where Have All the Workers Gone?

Taxes are just one area that highlights the adverse impact of the small Generation X following the giant Boomer generation. Another critically affected area is America's labor force.

The vast majority of our labor force of 140 million people is between twenty and sixty years old. In round numbers, those currently between twenty and forty, called Generation X, represent 45 percent of the total workforce. Those between forty and sixty, the Baby Boomers, make up 55 percent of the workforce. This differential doesn't seem all that great, but if you look a little deeper, as I've told you over and over, you will see that *Boomers outnumber Xers by nine million people.* That 11 percent difference is already creating a profound labor shortage at key levels of the workforce—from fast-food managers to skilled technicians to mid-level corporate executives.

Does Anyone Speak English?

I remember going into a McDonald's restaurant about ten years ago and ordering a double cheeseburger. I really don't like McDonald's food, but it was convenient and I was hungry and, to its credit, the food is consistent. It's about a three or four on a scale of ten, whether you buy it in Paris or San Diego. I don't like any extras on my double cheeseburgers, so this requires a little diligence when ordering: "I would like a double cheeseburger plain and a small Diet Coke, please."

Experience had taught me that this simple wording would get me what I wanted about nine out of ten times. In this particular case, I got a blank stare. "I just want a plain double cheeseburger without ketchup, onions, pickles, or mustard." The stare became more vacant and a conference in Spanish ensued behind the counter. Others joined in, including a manager-looking type, but the resolution did not come until we employed sign language. I was not in Mexico City. I was on Interstate 95 in Connecticut.

This begs the question: Why had McDonald's staffed this restaurant with a non–English speaking help when 95 percent of its customers spoke only English? Answer? It had no choice. The huge bell-shaped curve of nearly eighty million Boomers had aged well out of the entry-level labor force that would have supplied McDonald's with an English-speaking staff. It was 1997 and it was Generation X's turn to supply entry-level labor.

The bad news for filling entry-level positions is the fact that *Generation X is about 11 percent smaller in critical mass than the Boomer generation.* And Gen Xers are fully employed doing more fun stuff than working at the bottom of the food chain in fast food. So McDonald's and other fast-food chains had to import its labor and radically automate to stay in business.

The good news, ten years later, is that Generation Y will be supplying English-speaking, homegrown, entry-level labor to fast-food restaurants in vast overflowing quantities. This is precisely why you might see blond, blue-eyed, English-speaking young women behind the counter at fast-food restaurants on your next visit. We have not seen this for twenty years.

Why the change? Supply and demand is the answer. There are now far more entry-level workers than there are entry-level jobs. Data from the United States Bureau of Labor Statistics shows that in the summer of 1999, 48 percent of U.S. teens had jobs. Only 37 percent had jobs in the summer of 2006. Supply and demand changes attitudes. Don't believe me? Think about it. It is amazing what we will do when we need to survive. Ask anyone who experienced the Depression.

Generation X and the Skilled Labor Force

In spring 2003, Deloitte & Touche published a white paper for the American Manufacturers Association stating that the United States will be ten million workers short of its needs in the skilled-labor category, starting now, with the shortage intensifying over the next twenty years.

Labor shortages are already apparent in many sectors, even with the specter of the 6 percent unemployment. Categories that are most obviously affected include the skilled trades: seamstresses, plumbers, carpenters, electricians, cabinetmakers, furniture makers, masons, construction workers, heavy-equipment operators, auto technicians, diesel technicians, auto-body specialists, longshoremen, truck drivers, bus drivers, marine technicians, boat builders, carpet layers, painters, roofers, landscapers, machinists, merchant mariners, heat and air-conditioning technicians, and assemblers and repair people of all categories.

The aforementioned represent shortages today. The need to fill these positions is acute, but will pale compared with the need that will loom if the U.S. economy strengthens. In fact, many people say that our economy could be crippled by an inability to get the work done when growth accelerates.

As Boomers begin to exit the labor force at about age fifty-five, the generation behind it cannot, by virtue of critical mass, take up the slack. Remember, *Generation X is fully 11 percent smaller than the Boomers in mass;* in addition, twice as many went to college, further exacerbating the shortage of people available for skilled labor.

The difference between what these two generations offer to the skilled labor force is staggering. The United States is facing a very, very serious issue. Where will this labor come from? Asia, Mexico, Central and South America, Africa? No. These nations simply do not have surplus labor forces with the skills needed. There is only one source of skilled labor that would be compatible with our needs. It's the European Union.

Simply stated, the European Union (E.U.) has trained a large part of its population for jobs that don't exist in their countries. Ironically, the skilled-labor environment in the E.U. is the inverse of the U.S. environment.

Before we decry immigration, we need to remember that immigrant workers pay income tax and yes (!) social security tax. Placing skilled laborers in the United States will benefit everyone. The E.U. won't have to pay unemployment costs. The United States will fill a labor shortage. A yet-to-emerge placement firm will reap massive rewards for itself and investors. Best of all, there will be a legion of people who get to have jobs.

American truck driving can illustrate the labor-shortage issue and the potential for a European solution.

Where Are All the Truck Drivers?

I hope I can shed some light on what I consider the real issue and cause for the unacceptable truck-safety problems on U.S. highways. I am a demographer. I study how the rise and fall of birthrates and populations affect commerce, culture, and economics. I can forecast how a product will sell based on the market or population that is aging toward it. In the late 1990s, I recognized that a truck-driver shortage of epic proportions would severely compromise truck safety. You see, between 1965 and 1984 the birth rate in the United States dropped dramatically, *over 11 percent*, as I keep telling you.

Truck driving is one of the largest employment categories in the nation. According to a December 2007 report from the Bureau of Labor Statistics, there were almost 3.4 million employed truckers on the road in 2006. The BLS projects the United States will need an additional 258,000 by 2016, for a total of 3.6 million. It is not attractive work and does not pay well. When the population-deficient Generation X became old enough to supply our entry-level truck drivers, there were few takers. The trucking industry has gone begging ever since. The industry is currently at least 250,000 drivers short of its needs.

Count the number of "driver wanted" ads in your local newspaper and you will get the picture. Payroll expenses for truck drivers are at an all-time high. This has resulted in relaxed hiring standards and deferred maintenance on the trucks—yes, brakes and tires! Couple this with drivers who are pushed to the limit, have drug issues, no training, often no licenses, and who are actually encouraged to speed, and you have an untenable situation.

So what is the solution? In 2003 I attempted to persuade the Bush administration to allow German truck drivers (the most trained and skilled in the world) to enter the United States on special visas. The German government actually offered to subsidize this process to help alleviate its enormous unemployment issues. George Bush was for the idea and spoke openly about European immigration in late 2003. Someone told me that Karl Rove shot the idea down, fearing an anti-immigration backlash that could cost the 2004 election. (How's that for shortsighted thinking?)

Eventually our own huge homegrown Generation Y will alleviate the driver shortage, but it is currently too young to solve the problem.

Where Have All the Managers Gone?

The labor shortage caused by the small number of Generation Xers trying to fill the footprint of the giant Boomer generation is not limited to skilled-labor jobs.

I spent the better part of a recent summer in Massachusetts consulting for a New England retailer with multiple stores in several states. One of the many problems we addressed was the difficulty finding and keeping good store managers. "They don't want to work," "You can't get them to stay," "They don't understand loyalty and responsibility"—I had heard it all before, but these comments had always described entry-level positions, not management positions. Guess what? The population deficit has marched forward in age.

What am I talking about? Generation X. That's right, Generation X is a very long way from the day it will stop causing interesting challenges and problems for the United States. In its forty-year history it has shut down maternity wards, put toy stores out of business, closed public schools, wiped out the Japanese motorcycle business in the U.S., and failed to provide enough entry-level labor to run McDonald's and Dunkin' Donuts. So what are Gen Xers doing now? They are choking the life out of midlevel management.

Generation Xers were born between 1965 and 1984. Remember there are about nine million fewer of them than the Boomers born 1945 to 1964. The huge Boomer population is about forty-four to sixty-three years old at this writing.

As the Boomers exit management positions, the Xers should move in. The problem is there are not enough Xers to fill the positions. This creates musical chairs in reverse. The Bureau of Labor Statistics forecasts that by 2012 there will be three to four million fewer workers than jobs. This shortage will be broad in scope, but nowhere will it be more acutely felt than in management. You can automate line work and use immigrants to fill entry-level positions, but management is a totally different story. You cannot run a business without management. If a business isn't managed, a business isn't going to be a business for very long.

This is a problem for any organization that relies on solid supervision and management. This includes municipal organizations like police departments. What happens when police departments can't find sergeants and lieutenants? (Ironically, the shortage does not include politicians. I don't know why.)

The American Management Association has recognized this issue. Midlevel management-training enrollment has dropped significantly over the past seven years. Why? My theory is that companies are competing for young managers by bidding up their salaries. This money has to be made up somewhere. They are just glad to have managers. Forget the training. For that matter, who can keep them on the job long enough to train them?

Please don't take my word for all this. Check with your human resources professionals and see if they are having difficulty filling midlevel management positions. Now you can tell them why.

The United States is the world's leading industrialized nation. We can ill afford to have this breakdown of management. So what is the answer? One answer might be to rethink management, forget about age discrimination, and rehire Boomers. Our client in Massachusetts could now have two (Boomer) managers per store with relaxed schedules and relaxed physical demands. They are punctual, loyal, seldom call in sick, and work hard. Life is good. Well, sort of.

I have probably hired a thousand people in my career, maybe more. They have come in all genders, nationalities, shapes, sizes, colors, persuasions, religions, and creeds. Historically my pattern for hiring followed a particular blueprint. By that I mean I would exercise a certain sequential thought process when I considered the open position, and then in my mind's eye I would envision the person with the appropriate qualifications needed to fill it. Those of you who work in human resources probably know what I am talking about.

Try a quick experiment. Think of a position that you need to fill in your own company or in a client's company. Now envision the person you need to fill that position. Got it? Can you see that person? Now, I am not clairvoyant, so I can't tell you what you see. But I think I can tell what a lot of you don't see. You don't see someone who is ugly, overweight, or old. I don't know why that is. I am guilty of that same bias.

Last spring, I was in the Manhattan office of the president of a major corporation. We were discussing the impending labor shortage. He told me that he had an administrative assistant position that he was having trouble filling. I asked him to describe that person to me off the record. I asked him, "Who do you see?" This is what he said: "She is about thirty to thirty-five, tall, thin, professional, very bright, and personable." He caught himself and said, "I am glad that was off the record." It is a good thing that his answer was off the record because that is discrimination and it is illegal. But in reality we all do it everyday. We are all bigoted in one way or another.

You notice that my company president did not say he saw a white woman. Why? Because, it would not matter to him if she was a Caucasian, African American, or Asian. He didn't care because race is not one of his biases. He just didn't want someone who was male, ugly, fat, or old. The person he described just happened to be at the very bottom of Generation X's labor force and was in very short supply. This president is going to have to rethink his biases and hire the most qualified person regardless of gender, appearance, and age.

Boomers to the Rescue?

The clear solution to this dramatic labor issue is the redeployment of a wonderful labor resource: the unemployed Baby Boomer. You see, a lot of very qualified Baby Boomers are victims of outsourcing, downsizing, right-sizing, and layoffs. They are easy targets. They are highly paid and have a lot of vacation time. They know "where the bodies are buried." Out they go. Costs are cut.

But no one bothered to analyze the available workforce to ensure that the young Xers could replace exiting Boomers. And the fact is the younger Xers can't replace the Boomers because there simply aren't enough of those Xers to go around.

This midlevel management shortage will intensify and cripple even healthy businesses. The problem is nationwide. All the human resources organizations that I work with ask me to address this. Ironically, the answer is right in front of our noses. We need to recycle the Boomers now. They are an extremely valuable resource that is ignored. A lot of them have given up looking for work and now face questionable retirements. The Boomers all tell me the same thing: "Try getting hired when you are over fifty." Boomers being recycled, it's a green thing . . . sort of.

The real bad news is the fact that Generation X has taken its devastating labor deficit and aged. A while ago I had an e-mail exchange with Sue Meisinger, the president and CEO of the Society for Human Resource Management (SHRM). This is a huge national association, probably the biggest that deals directly with human resource issues. She used the phrase "perfect storm" to describe the impending talent shortage facing the United States. "Perfect storm" is not good.

Ms. Meisinger further explained that she and her colleagues had been aware of this looming crisis for some time and knew that the real issue was shifting demography. They even had a nationally famous demographer and generational marketer, Ken Dychtwald, speak at their annual meeting about a year ago.

What is striking here is the fact that Sue Meisinger and her constituents get it. They are anticipating a problem and (gasp!) preparing for it. I cannot say the same for the C-level executives at Wal-Mart or General Motors.

So what does all this mean? Well, in simple terms, we will not have enough people to run business and industry as we know it. On the bright side, the need for people in the skilled technical trades will eventually (within ten years) be satisfied by Generation Y, which is filling public technical schools with the best candidates they have seen in twenty years. The real long-term issue will be the shortage of mid- to upper-level nontechnical talent and management. The shortage of management has the potential to cripple commerce and even government, because you can't run a successful company or organization without good management. This, of course, points out the incredible importance of successful recruitment and retention, which could lead the way to the human resources department's finest hour. Companies and organizations will compete for human capital more intensely than they compete for sales or results. Talent will be at a premium like never before. This should move human resources into C-level prominence with ease if the CEOs and boards of directors wake up in time. However, all bets are off and nothing can stay the same.

The human resources department itself is not immune, so you can expect dramatic fallout when Boomers bail out because of the increased pressure to perform. Human resources will need to market itself and its organizations in a new way. Today's communications and attitudes ("Applications now being taken") will need to be abandoned and replaced with professional, effective, competitive persuasion at every level. It's a new ball game.

CHAPTER 18

The Gen X Labor Shortage and the Impact on Direct Mail

I love mail. As a result of this passion, I read everything that's put into my mailbox. I love freestanding inserts (flyers), too. Some people call this stuff "junk mail." I don't! Over my years in the marketing business, I have produced literally billions of individual pages that have found their way into people's homes.

A while back, I received a mail piece that stopped me dead in my tracks. It was a 5- by 8-inch postcard printed in one color. The sender was our local post office. The riveting message was simple: The post office was taking applications for mail carriers. You might say, "Yeah, so what?" But this was the first time I had ever seen an ad to recruit mail carriers.

Why is this significant? It's significant because throughout the past thirty years there has been a waiting list for anyone wanting to become a postal carrier. That piece of mail told me that mail carriers have now joined the ranks of other trades such as fire fighters, police, nurses, mechanics, carpenters, electricians, plumbers, truck drivers, and everyone else we used to call "blue collar." Welcome to the club, Mr. and Ms. Postmaster. Prepare to start begging for help. And guess what? It's only going to get worse.

So, what does all this mean to direct marketers? Gulp! The cost of producing our product is going to go up—way up. First, printing prices will escalate because there are no pressman apprentices. That's what I said, none. Printers will have to pay more for printing talent.

Shipping prices also will skyrocket. As I told you in chapter 17, the United States is currently 250,000 truck drivers short of its current needs. As the economy improves, we will see this shortage get worse.

Let's look at trucking for a minute. Think about the number of truck accidents you hear about in your area and then consider how hard this dwindling labor pool is being pushed to get goods delivered. Clearly, there are many people on the road driving trucks who should not be on the road. The government is only going to allow this condition to exist for so long before we have a major crackdown and enforcement of trucking regulations. All of this spells higher costs.

Postage has to go up because the U.S. Postal Service is going to have to pay more to attract workers, and it is very reliant on the trucking industry. What's this all going to cost us? Do the math. We could be looking at double our present costs. That's the bad news.

Is there good news for direct marketers? Yes. Commercial mass media (radio, television, and print) are losing their audiences and shooting themselves in the foot by raising prices and running more ads. There is no TiVo for direct mail. By the way, don't you just love TiVo? Where else but in the United States could a company thrive by selling a device and technology that enables consumers to cripple a sixty-year-old commercial model and essentially steal entertainment and information from its originators?

In this country, we have a time-honored tradition of paying for radio and television with our time and attention as we endure commercials. I hope the TiVo folks realize that once they wipe out our current form of commercial television, they are out of business, too.

As long as the nation has mailboxes, direct mail has a future. And even the most devoted Internet followers check their "snail mail." Direct marketers could be the last and most effective means of reaching audiences of this century.

Finally, consider the twentysomethings of Generation Y. This generation will be the largest and most actively consuming generation in history. Generation Y is already the same size as the Boomers and growing. Before this generation is done in 2010, it will be 100 million strong and have an appetite for consumption five times stronger than Boomers had at comparable ages in adjusted dollars.

Direct marketers and their companies will be the clear winners in the decades to come—no matter what happens to costs, labor, and the generational shifts that lay ahead. Direct marketing will reach Generation Y like no other medium can.

CHAPTER 19

Case Study

How Generation X Drove Motorcycle Sales off the Cliff

When a market of Generation Xers follows a market of Boomers, the sixty-nine million Gen Xers enter a gaping hole emptied by seventy-eight million incredibly hungry, thirsty, consuming people. In other words, when Gen X comes along, we're missing *nine million buyers.*

Any 11 percent free fall in a market vaporizes that market. That's what happened to motorcycles (see Figure 19.1). In 1979, my company won a regional American Honda Motorcycle advertising account. It was one of our first nationally recognized clients and the source of great pride to the agency. In

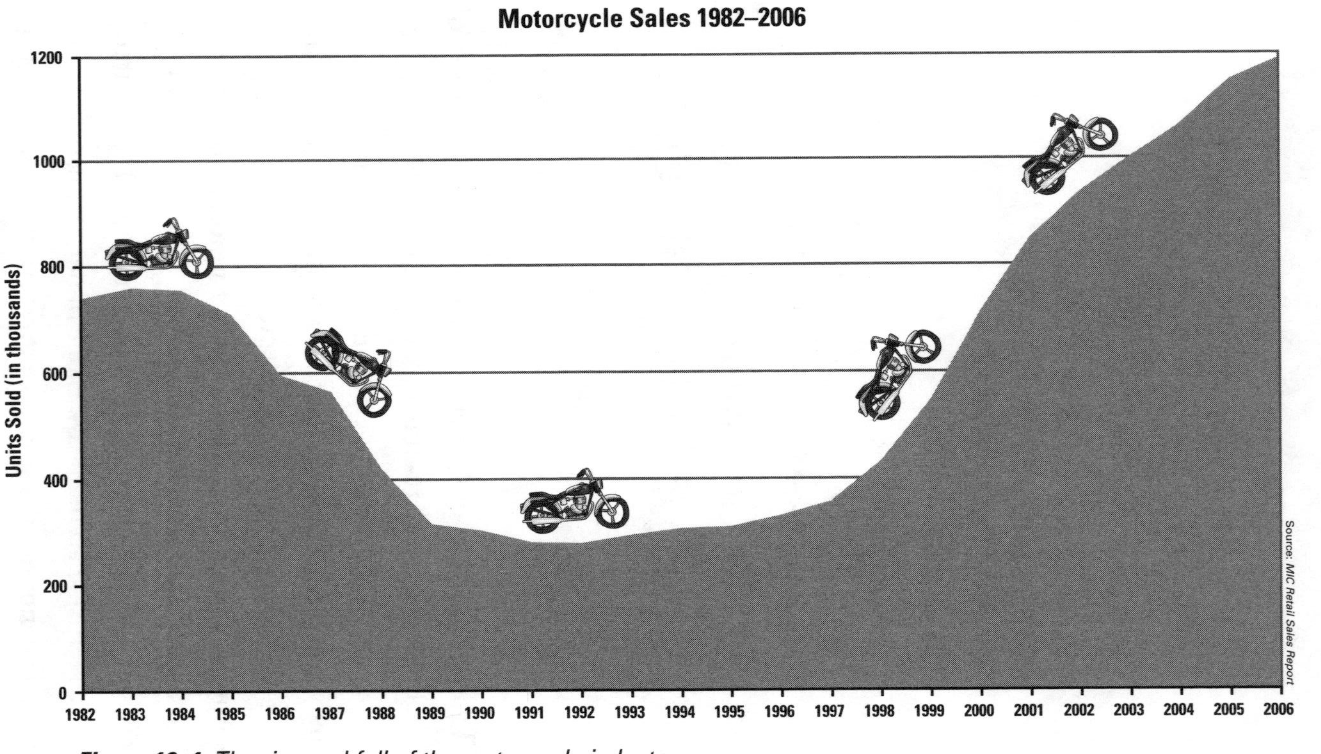

Figure 19–1. *The rise and fall of the motorcycle industry*

that year, Honda was selling roughly 400,000 units per year with a 40 percent share of the market.

The number of individual Honda motorcycle dealerships we served grew from 30 to 130 in just a few years, covering Maine to Pittsburgh to Washington, D.C. The relationship was great. Bikes were flying out the door and cash registers were ringing. Sales had spiked after *Easy Rider*, and we saw them spike again with the release of *Top Gun*. Tom Cruise's mantra, "The need for speed," did wonders for the Japanese motorcycle market. Our marketing couldn't make a mistake, even if we tried. We were geniuses. Life was good.

But in 1986 sales came to a screeching halt; 1987 was not any better; 1988 was worse; 1989 showed no improvement. We began to sense a pattern. What are we doing wrong? We all scratched our heads.

> *"When a market the size of Generation X follows a market of Boomers, the sixty-nine million Gen Xers enter a gaping hole emptied by seventy-eight million incredibly hungry, thirsty, consuming people. In other words, when Gen X comes along, we're missing* ***nine million buyers.****"*

Initially, people blamed the dramatic drop-off on the design of the 1986 models. After the alleged flaw was corrected, however, sales still headed south. Meanwhile, American Honda continued to ship the previous year's dealer-shipments quantity plus 10 percent more, as per the dealer franchise agreement. Somehow it saw no problem with this. As far as Honda was concerned, once the bikes were shipped to the dealers *they were sold.* Things were fine.

It took a while for Honda to recognize that something was wrong—and, more important, to respond. I remember Honda sending a select contingent of Japanese executives to the United States to study the problem firsthand sometime in the early 1990s. By this time, it was all over but the crying; the dealers were, nevertheless, happy that Honda was finally doing something.

After coming to grips with the fact that there was a serious problem going well beyond a single year's model, the experts from Honda concluded that the problem was that the bikes were overpriced. I was just a marketing guy, but I knew that price was only an issue between the dealers themselves because they discounted the bikes in an effort to get sales away from other Honda dealers. This was the typical price war that routinely takes place when there are more products than customers. I knew that the problem was more fundamental than the price of the bikes because Suzuki, Yamaha, and Kawasaki were all having identical problems and the price of similar bikes varied dramatically. I did not, however, have an answer, so I took my place among those who deferred to the experts from Honda.

Honda's strategy was simple. It produced a special edition of its signature product, the best-selling Honda Nighthawk

750, and reduced its price by one-third. This motorcycle was a staple in the lineup and was the motorcycle that launched Honda into the big leagues in the early 1970s. It sold for $5,999. Honda drastically reduced the price to $3,999. To my knowledge, that's never been done before in the automotive industry. It was a lot of bike for the money. We advertised everywhere. We pulled out the entire arsenal of advertising tools including print, radio, TV, and billboards. There were spectacular promotions and test-drive campaigns. How many were sold? Only a few. The glory days were over.

This mysterious plague on the market wiped 130 dealerships down to just a handful. Sales fell by 80 percent by the mid-1990s, from 400,000 units to 80,000. Finally, with all the marketing analysts and MBAs looking like deer in the headlights, everyone shook hands and parted.

I still wonder why the MBAs were scratching their heads. Don't they learn about supply and demand at business school? I don't have an MBA, so I expect MBAs to be smarter than me. That's fair, isn't it?

What Happened?

So do you want to know why it all happened? If not, you can skip to Chapter 20.

Who buys Japanese motorcycles? Men do. (Women are a *growing* market for motorcycles, especially Harley-Davidsons, but their overall numbers remain small compared with men.)

How old are these men? They are sixteen to twenty-four years old. That's it, period. At twenty-five, they're not in the market anymore. Why? Because at twenty-six they get married. They often need to buy an expensive piece of jewelry called an engagement ring. Today's brides expect at least a one-carat diamond. Where do these guys get the money? They sell their motorcycles. It is amazing how close in price a late-model high-end Japanese motorcycle is in price to a one-carat diamond ring.

Even if the men don't sell their motorcycles to buy rings, there is something else at work here. Girlfriends tolerate motorcycles. It might have something to do with the exciting outlaw persona associated with men who ride motorcycles. That works in attracting, not keeping, mates. Young wives, and especially young mothers, hate motorcycles. They are a real and proven threat to everything a young woman wants from marriage.

High-performance Japanese motorcycles can do zero to sixty in three seconds. You can buy a Japanese motorcycle that goes over 200 miles an hour. I once watched a Suzuki Hayabusa rider taunt a Connecticut State Police cruiser on westbound Interstate 84. He would wait until the cruiser caught up and then would pull the bike up on one wheel and accelerate like nothing I have ever seen. The cop finally backed off and let him go. Police cars cannot catch these motorcycles and for the most part don't even try. U.S. roads are also not designed for those speeds.

The chances of dying on a Japanese motorcycle are very high because of the way people ride them. The chances of being maimed are even higher. The motorcycle is the most unsafe form of conventional transportation there is, and it happens to be in the hands of the most unsafe group, which thinks it is invincible. Add alcohol and drugs to this mix and you have a lot of dead and severely injured young men. So it's no wonder that after an engagement, the first thing to go is this death-wish vehicle.

It is important to note that motorcycles fall into three basic categories that appeal to different age groups. Japanese superbikes appeal to sixteen- to twenty-four-year-olds. Motocross or off-road bikes have a broader age appeal because they are part of an organized sport that can be enjoyed by kids as young as ten who often ride with their dads. Harley-Davidson motorcycles and all their Japanese clones appeal to an older group of thirty- to sixty-year-olds who are content to make a lot of noise, raise money for charity, and ride very slowly.

Once the peak of Boomer men aged past the sixteen- to twenty-four-year-old prime Japanese-motorcycle-buying age, the number of Japanese bikes sold fell by 80 percent. Do the math. In 1986 the last of those Boomers born from 1957 to 1961 (the magic five-year peak) turned twenty-six. By 1993 the Boomer generation had completely moved on. Generation X moved into the Japanese-motorcycle-buying age and snuffed the life out of it for twenty years.

A Lesson in Retail Math

I was once asked at a presentation how Generation X, being only 11 percent smaller than the Boomer generation, can possibly wipe out a market established by the larger generation that precedes it. It kind of surprised me. I thought everyone knew that a 5 percent drop in market size was disastrous, especially to franchise businesses that for the most part are all the same.

My accountant always told me that a 5 percent after-tax profit was very healthy for a small business. He explained that the last five sales out of 100 we made were the ones where we got to keep *all* of the money. This was a revelation to me, an epiphany. It was at that point I understood the value of *every* customer. If I lost only one customer out of 100, that was 20 percent of my profit (because that was one of the five customers who were profitable). If I lost five customers out of 100, I would have zero profit. Our Honda motorcycle dealers had lost eleven customers out of a hundred, so there was no profit and they were running deep into the red.

Keep in mind too that we are comparing overall generation size over a twenty-year time frame. In other words, the 11 percent difference is an *average* over time. The real differences between Generation X and the Boomers could easily be measured by the percentage differences between the Boomers' peak and Generation X's valley. At the peak of the Boomers' fertility, Boomers were producing 4.3 million live births per year. At the bottom of Generation X's productivity, only 3.3

million live births were recorded. That is a free fall of just under 25 percent.

However we do the math, the implications are devastating. There is a saying in the retail business: "Retail is detail." What does it mean? It means that retail is a game of subtleties and the difference between success and failure is often very subtle and often very small. In retail, an 11 percent free fall in the size of your market is disastrous.

I know it would be logical to say, "Why not just downsize your overhead by 15 percent overall and be fine?" It doesn't work that way in retail. First, it is hard to downsize without negatively affecting your product, service, and company morale. Second, the first casualty of a market downturn is advertising because it is easy to cut. Also, advertising does not work very well in a shrinking market, because the best you can hope for is to be predatory and this often involves deep discounts. Thus, the downward spiral begins. Sometimes strong independent competitors can survive a market downturn, but in the case of the Honda motorcycle dealers, their franchise with Honda essentially made them all one business.

Fast Forward to Today

A new day is dawning. Honda's problems began when the peak Baby Boomers exited the defined sixteen- to twenty-four-year-old male demo beginning in 1986. The demographic shift caught the Japanese (and just about everybody else) by surprise.

Now it looks like the Japanese motorcycle industry in general and Honda in particular are going to get caught flatfooted again, but for the opposite reasons.

When you visit a Honda motorcycle dealership (the few that are left), you will see that Honda has made a concerted effort to clone Harley-Davidson's anachronistic motorcycle concept, evidenced by all the Harley look-alikes on the showroom floor. It's sad. The bloom is off the rose for Harley-Davidson and all its Japanese copies. Harley-Davidsons and Harley-Davidson clones are Boomer bikes made for the Boomer market. Boomers are aging out of the market and once again Generation X is not going to pick up the slack. It can't.

The market of the future is looking for the super-high-performance café racer bike. This is the bike that will bring members of Generation Y into the showrooms *if it is marketed to them.* My advice to Honda and the other Japanese brands is: What are you waiting for?! If this opportunity were any bigger, it would bite you! This market is ready now and it has the potential to dwarf the sales numbers you saw in the seventies and eighties. Based on the sheer consumption of *stuff* by Generation Y, I cannot see any reason why motorcycle sales couldn't double compared with the Boomer consumption in the seventies and eighties.

So, what's up? The Japanese car guys get it. They are going after the Generation Y market with a vengeance. The Subaru WRX and the Mitsubishi eVO are good examples of "Boy Racers" from the factory. Japanese car manufacturers have apparently carefully studied how Generation Y customizes its own cars and then translated this into new car design. This is a page right out of Lee Iacocca's book. Iacocca did the same thing with the Mustang forty years ago.

If the Japanese automakers can do it, Honda and other motorcycle makers can do it. The marketing story should be simple and very visceral. These bikes are all about power, speed, and mystique. For young men, this is about coming of age on two wheels. In addition to strategically placed television ads with very high production values, over-the-top talent, and contemporary music, I would blanket YouTube with renegade video stories to create an urban legend about my product.

> *"I still wonder why the MBAs were scratching their heads. Don't they learn about supply and demand at business school?"*

CHAPTER 20

Case Study
Planes Stuck on the Ground—A Business Traveler's Tale

Some companies just don't get it. When they finally do get it, it's too late because not getting it has already put them into Chapter 11. Most of us don't have the luxury of allowing experience to be the teacher. When we make mistakes and lose customers, they're gone.

Consider the airline industry. If you ask any airline executive why his carrier has problems, he'll tell you 9/11 did it in. In one way it did do the carriers in. But their issues started long before 9/11. The real problems of the airline industry go back to the early '90s when Generation X began traveling for business. The 9/11 attacks simply finished a job that began with very poor marketing, woeful customer service, nonexistent research, and unfavorable demography. What happened?

"The guy was friendly enough. He and the wife were going to play the slots. They bought two round-trip tickets for only $149 each. Great. I paid $1,400."

I recently pondered that question on a flight to Las Vegas. I didn't want to make this last-minute business trip, but I had to appear at an apparel show. The trip required me to get up in the middle of the night, drive to the airport, park the car, struggle with my luggage, get on and off the shuttle bus, struggle with my luggage again, pay off the Sky Cap, wait in more lines, set off the metal detector, get frisked and interrogated, find my way to the gate for a delayed flight, and then finally board and sit next to a guy in a Hawaiian shirt who really needed an extra seat.

The guy was friendly enough. He and the wife were going to play the slots. They bought two round-trip tickets for only $149 each. Great. I paid $1,400.

Okay, so I bought my tickets the day before and he bought his months before. So punish me. I was stupid. I should've known better and planned ahead. In this case, I couldn't do that. So this was my fault. But that argument didn't help me. His seat was the same as mine. He ate the same stupid snacks (is it me, or does air travel make you hungry and lower your standards?). We were on the same plane. We bought the same product from the same seller. The difference is that I paid 839 percent more than he did for something I really did not like to do.

About Business Travel

Business travel is not fun. And it is definitely not a perk. However, it is the profit center for the airline industry. So what do the airlines do with their "Best Customers?" They grossly overcharge them. I must have missed the logic.

Without business travelers, an airline cannot function, because that is where the money is. Without business travelers, big guys in Hawaiian shirts can't fly to Las Vegas for $149 round-trip. Strange as it seems, this absurd marketing formula would have continued to work had it not been for the 11 percent free fall in market size between Boomers and Xers.

Aside from the fact that the customer base has shrunk, we're seeing a new mentality in the way people view jobs. Xers started looking for work and discovered that they were in demand. For every ten lower-level executive jobs the Boomers left, there were only nine Xers ready to step in and replace them.

Xers have been called arrogant children because they can afford to be arrogant and get away with it. They are in short supply, like the males in the famous Jan and Dean song "Surf City." Even if you're ugly, in Surf City you can get a date. Even the ugly Xers got jobs.

Here's the rub for the airline industry: Jobs that required 50 percent-plus travel went begging because business travel is not a perk. It is a hassle. Especially air travel.

This phenomenon could be called the "graying of air travel." I watched it happen in the days when I traveled frequently. I made a game of spotting the business-traveling Xers. This wasn't easy because there were so few of them. Boomers endured the pain of air travel because they had to put up with it. Xers refused and got away with it. Businesses began to promote more Internet contact, virtual meetings, and phone conferences.

> *"Business travel is not fun. And it is definitely not a perk. However, it is the profit center for the airline industry. So what do the airlines do with their 'Best Customers'? They grossly overcharge them. I must have missed the logic."*

Once there seemed to be no substitute for the face-to-face meeting. Now they are rare, especially if they require air travel. Businesses actually have saved a ton of money, and they work faster and more efficiently without sending their people all over the globe.

Generation Y to the Rescue

Airlines will begin to catch a break as Generation Y begins to flood the workforce. This forecast might be a bit premature but, hey, I'm a futurist. Heavy travel as a requirement for work is not a perk but a deterrent. No one wants to spend his or her life in the air or in hotels. When Generation X entered the workforce, it shunned jobs requiring undesirable heavy travel because it could, and it could because there were more jobs than applicants. With Gen Y the exact opposite is true. The jobs requiring heavy travel will have all the eager Gen Y applicants they need because the tables have been turned. Now there will be many more applicants than jobs. So you can expect to see the very profitable business-travel part of air-travel spike. This should start soon and continue to grow until further notice. Look for young faces in the aisle seats. This is very good news for the airlines, because business travelers pay much more for their seats than vacationers (as I noted).

However, airlines still have some work to do. The name "air bus" comes to mind as a metaphor for air travel. Airlines would do well to distance themselves from the idea of a bus. Bus travel and air travel should be worlds apart; they shouldn't even be in the same sentence. The airlines need to sell the experience of air travel and make the experience as much fun for the traveler as getting to the location. Airlines also need to make the experience a productive time for the business traveler. There is a major disconnect in the delivery of the air travel product when no attention is paid to the amount spent on the ticket. My advice to airlines: Take care of your business travelers. They are your profit. There is no better time to rebrand your product and change your delivery than right now, because your new market, Generation Y, has no preconceived ideas about you or air travel. *Make Generation Y love flying* and you will print money.

For example, members of Generation Y are natives in the cyberworld. Members of older generations are immigrants. Generation Y loves electronic gadgets, especially as they relate to communication. If you have ever seen a teen use his or her phone to send a text message, you know what I mean. I would recommend that airlines accommodate their new Generation Y business travelers with on-plane Internet access and in-flight chatrooms so passengers can access each other. I am not sure how this would be achieved electronically, but that doesn't matter. With today's technology, if you can think it, it is doable.

I cannot tell you of the number of important contacts I have made on planes when I have had the good fortune of sitting next to a person who could help me with my business. I have found both customers and suppliers. Now multiply this opportunity by the number of people on the plane, and flying becomes a networking opportunity of the highest order. This would work and Generation Y would love it.

However, instead of making business travel more pleasant and productive, airlines have cut more corners, delivered a lesser product, and driven everyone away except the big guy in the Hawaiian shirt.

CHAPTER 21

Case Study
The Death of a Discount Store

It was the eleventh hour, but worth a shot. We secured an appointment with the marketing department at Ames Discount Stores in Rocky Hill, Connecticut. We would review the principal tenets of generational marketing and possibly help them through a spiraling decline in their business.

Before the meeting, we visited a number of their stores to get a lay of the land and develop some talking points. Theirs was a similar format to K-Mart, but it was apparent that the market Ames sought was closer to the working poor and generally the bottom of the retail pecking order. But this wasn't a valid reason for poor sales. On close inspection, we found the underlying cause of the company's imminent sinking into the sea of red ink.

From a demographic standpoint, the product mix was completely out of alignment with expanding pie markets. Ames had aggressively chosen instead to pursue shrinking, overserved markets that warranted competing solely on price.

To our way of thinking Ames had chosen, and pursued, exactly the wrong path. The irony is that this strategy would have worked fifteen to twenty years earlier. When a market moves toward your product or service, the sales process is very forgiving. New, growing markets are always underserved, and quite often just having a product needed by the new market is enough reason for it to sell. In contrast, a shrinking market is always overserved and companies wage the battle for remaining customers on price alone. Guess which one is more fun and profitable?

> *"First marriages will remain light for at least another ten years until Gen Ys start to tie the knot. Boomers, on their second and third marriages, already have all the stuff they need."*

We found that there were three big problems with what Ames was doing.

1. The bulk of Ames' business was aimed at young couples and those setting up first-time households. The problem here

was the fact that though the number of marriages at the time was still quite high in the United States, the number of first marriages had dropped like a stone. *That's because there are 11 percent fewer people in Generation X than are in the previous Boomer generation.* First marriages will remain very light for at least another five years until Gen Ys start to tie the knot. Boomers, on their second and third marriages, already have all the stuff they need.

2. Problem number two was evident in the Ames toy department. Toys dominated 20 percent of the floor space, but 80 percent of the inventory was for young children under ten. At that time, the peak of Gen Y had already passed the stuffed-animal stage by two years. Hence, Ames had chosen once again to compete in a shrinking market. Kids twelve and over do not want stuffed animals at any price.

3. The final problem was a classic. Ames was going after the elderly with a vengeance. It was creating marketing campaigns and offering discounts directly to the geriatrics. It aimed to capture the "Graying of America." Only no one had told Ames about that Grand Canyon of generations: The tiny Silent Generation, which was positioned between the GI Generation and the Boomers. *Strike three.*

We presented our case, but I could tell by the blank stares that they were not buying it. What we heard was, "If it worked fifteen years ago it will work today." Bye, Bye, Miss American Pie.

Once again, retail is detail. You really have to do everything right to make a go of it. I have had the pleasure to work with some wonderful retailers and together we created some wild success stories.

One of our ad agency's hallmark clients was a regional New England apparel store by the name of Bob's Stores. We began working with Bob's when its sales were $10 million. We worked together for twenty years until sales crested $400 million. It was a wonderful ride. If someone asked me what made Bob's such an enormous success, I would say that the folks at Bob's listened to us. They paid for expert advice and then they took it to heart. They also hired exceptional people and then let them do their jobs. This is rare today. It was the legacy of Bob's Stores late founder, Bob Lapidus.

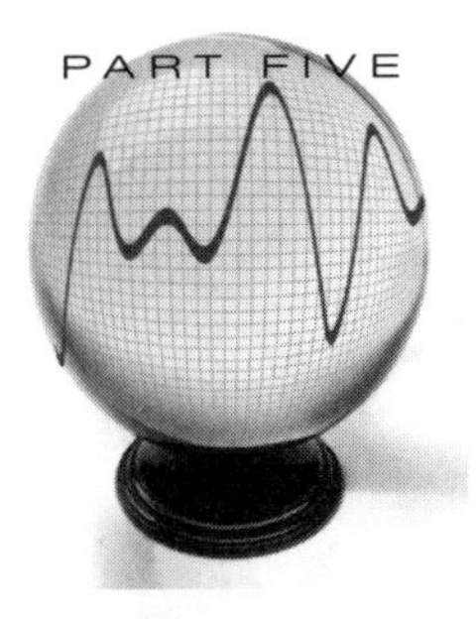

Generation Y

The Giant on the Horizon

C H A P T E R 22

Stop Looking in the Rearview Mirror!

When I attended California State University at Long Beach, I was an avid follower and fan of Marshall McLuhan, author of such classics as *The Global Village* and *The Medium Is the Message.* McLuhan stated that we live in a rearview mirror world.

What did he mean? He meant that we don't know where we are; we only know where we have been. As we live our lives, we tend to make decisions based on where we have been, not where we are, and certainly not on where we are going. Do you want to know how scary a thought that is?

Imagine that you are driving a car and your only point of reference is your rearview mirror. The front and side windows are blacked out. Can you still drive? Sort of, if you are on a wide-open interstate with no other cars. But most of us would simply choose to stop or occasionally be towed along by someone else.

When the Japanese motorcycle manufacturers watched sales explode as the Boomers entered the motorcycle-buying age in the late sixties, they made a deadly assumption. The assumption? Sales at this level would continue forever. They continued to open dealerships and expand their production and distribution right up until the sky fell. They saw the market through a rearview mirror and assumed that's what lay ahead.

Thinking from hearts and stomachs instead of numbers, marketers say, "We've been successful. Let's keep on building. There's just some sort of a marketplace anomaly. Sales will be back. Boomers love motorcycles and Levi's!"

However, marketers should watch for the market that's *increasing* in size, not the one getting smaller, even if they really love the one that's getting smaller. *Only the Baby Boomer Generation and Generation Y are delivering future expanding markets.* More people (Boomers) were born in 1957 (4.3 million) than in any other year in our nation's history. Actually 1957–1961 were huge defining years—years with live births above four million. Generation Y peaked in 1990 with about 4.2 million live births. It then dropped slightly to maintain at about four million per year for eighteen years and holding.

The peak years for the Boomers are important because the birthrate climbed significantly on the front side and then fell off dramatically afterward. It is not so important for Generation Y, because although the ramp up was steep, the plateau is flat and steady.

Thus, if you are currently selling to these two markets, make sure that your product and service is staying in front of the age curve as it is advancing. If you are selling Japanese motorcycles to Generation Y, for example, your future is bright and getting brighter. Japanese bikes sell to young men sixteen to twenty-four. The peak of Generation Y is about eighteen years old (that is, the peak of the Gen Y birthrate curve was eighteen years ago), and there is a sea of future riders behind them for the next twenty years.

If you are selling Harleys to Boomers, you might want to cash in your chips because the leading edge of the Boomers is currently sixty-three years old and the Boomer peak is fifty years old as of this writing. From my perspective, this is a saturated market that cannot get any bigger. If you want to see what is going to happen to the Harley market, take a look at Figure 19.1 in Chapter 19 for a refresher of what happened to the Japanese motorcycle market between 1986 and 1992. *The curse of the diminutive Generation X!*

In the years to come, and given the numbers and ages of the Boomers, Gen Xers, and Gen Yers during these years, here are some markets to embrace and some to avoid.

A Future You Can Taste

Let's begin with food. I think supermarket sales should be fine, but the way food is packaged will have to change. Generation Y is the emerging market for food stores. This generation doesn't know how to cook and probably won't learn. As a result, prepared foods will reach new levels of quality, light-years above TV dinners. Prepared entrees and precooked foods are going to need to be packaged better. Whole Foods is on the right track as far as wholesome ingredients are concerned, and its prepared entrees are excellent. But I think that Generation Y is going to push the envelope even further. For example, Generation Y women are shrinking away from meat in a big way. I think fish and chicken are safe for now. But red meat's days are numbered.

A few short years ago I was in Arkansas speaking in an amphitheater filled with Tyson Chicken executives at Tyson's headquarters. The occasion stands out in my mind because it was a long drive on very rural back roads to get to Tyson's offices, and I wondered where all these well-dressed, sophisticated executive types came from or where they lived. (Okay, so I am mired in a rural South stereotype.) The issue on the table was whether to acquire a red-meat processing plant for over $10 billion. It would give Tyson total dominance of supermarket meat cases.

As a demographic marketing expert, I advised Tyson against the purchase. Generation Y was already trending away from red-meat consumption with a vengeance; many were even becoming vegans. I maintained that if kids somehow make the connection that a McDonald's hamburger has its origins in a live steer, it could be over for McDonald's. Teen girls not only will not buy red meat, they won't even touch uncooked meat of any kind. Going forward, this posed some interesting challenges for the traditional supermarket meat case.

In addition, the peak of the Baby Boomers would be cresting fifty soon and losing their appetites. Don't believe me? Count the number of Boomers sharing plates in restaurants. The older you get the less fuel you need, period. In the long term, there is nowhere for red-meat consumption to go but down.

Tyson pulled the plug and the *Wall Street Journal* announced four days later that Tyson was backing out of the deal. The meat-processing entity alleged that the deal was already done, sued Tyson, and won. To exacerbate this situation further, the grain they feed to cows is now being used to manufacture fuel for cars, thus driving the cost of grain through the roof. The red-meat division of Tyson is slowly but surely pulling the company down.

The amount of money we spend on food in the United States is split about down the middle on food for home consumption (supermarkets) and food consumed out of the home (restaurants). These two have been jockeying for position and dominance for years. A few years ago, I thought the restaurants were going to win, but then the supermarkets came back with a one-two punch of prepared and whole foods. Now restaurants are firing back with quality food to go that includes convenient special parking right in front of the restaurant.

The National Restaurant Association states that sales of out-of-home food more than doubled between 1990 and 2007. The Bureau of Labor statistics puts at-home food expenditures at about 25 percent greater than expenditures on away-from-home food. Total food expenditures are about $650 billion. My gut tells me that restaurants are going to take a hit as Boomers opt for comforts and entertainment available in the home. Generation Y will spend money on restaurant food, but it will all be fast food. Generation Y will not spend serious money in restaurants for another ten years.

Clothing the Future

What about the clothing market? Clothing is plumage. We use clothing to attract the opposite sex, so it would follow that the clothing market is very dependent on the number of people looking for mates. I am not talking about Boomers' second and third marriages. Historically, in the United States we look for mates when we are between the ages of twenty-four and about thirty-four. Generation X still has a firm hold on this demographic landscape, but get ready: Generation Y is closing in fast. When Generation Y begins to fill the clothes-buying sweet spot, clothing sales are going to soar. I really do mean soar.

When clothing sales soar, so does fashion. Fashion is always the first casualty of poor clothing sales. No one wants to manufacture anything new, because the risk is too high, so manufacturers tend to stay with the basics. Think about it: Generation Xers all dress and look like warmed-over Boomers. The clothing market fell off a cliff when Boomers exited the peak clothes-buying age.

The Silent Generation dressed just like GI Generation. The members of Generation Y are spenders—big spenders—so there is no reason to believe that they are not going to consume fashionable clothing with a passion. This fact is going to have a significant effect on the clothing industry.

Currently, big-box retailers own the clothing market, but that is about to change. Wal-Mart sells a lot of clothes, but it doesn't sell a lot of fashion. Why? First, it doesn't have to. The people who buy the most clothes weren't making big fashion demands on the clothing industry and the clothing industry wasn't offering much selection of fashion. This was great for Wal-Mart and fit its retail model perfectly. It could buy this limited selection of clothes cheap and deep (in huge quantities) from China and sell them for less than anyone. Remember that buying from China does have some built-in rules. You need to limit your selection and you can't be in a hurry, because shipping time and cost is a factor.

So where is the big change? Generation Y's initial impact on the clothing market will come in the next couple of years in the form of a sales spike. This will precipitate an explosion in new fashion. Fashion turns fast and seldom calls for an endless supply. By the time Wal-Mart and other big-box stores wake up to what's in fashion, Generation Y will have moved on. So much for the cheap and deep retail model that pervades the clothing market. It will be history. So much for Wal-Mart.

Expect to see the equivalent of what we used to call "fashion boutiques" pop up everywhere just like they did in the 1970s to accommodate the Boomers' fashion demands. These fashion boutiques will be single stores and some small chains that will sell clothes made by boutique manufacturers that make their esoteric products here in the United States and probably Mexico. These small businesses will be a remarkable economic engine for the United States. Don't you just love Generation Y?

It's Early to Bed for the Boomers

One surprising area of growth will be the high-end mattress market, thanks to Boomers like me. I can't sleep. I wake up two or three times a night to use the bathroom and raid the refrigerator. My wife has a problem sleeping as well, but she doesn't get up. She just complains and blames the problem on our $2,000 mattress. "It's worn out," she says. It looks fine to me. In fact, it looks new when the sheets are stripped off. She makes me stoop down and look across the top of the mattress where she sees an invisible indentation. "See that? That's the problem," she states with conviction. I can see another mattress purchase on the horizon. Why me?

We are leading-edge Boomers who are entering the "can't sleep" age. The mattress manufacturers have been waiting for us. Our next mattress will not cost $2,000. It will cost $5,000. My wife and I will have our own "sleep numbers" and our own remote controls to adjust firmness and other things. My wife is convinced this will be the answer to our sleeping problems. I really hope this is the solution, because five large is a lot of money.

The bedding and mattress industry has been brought low by the intrepid yet diminutive Generation X. It is a familiar pattern. The huge Boomer population drives up the bedding/mattress production, distribution, and retail infrastructure, only to be followed by the smaller Generation X that torpedoes sales.

Fortunately for the bedding and mattress market, the Boomers who can't sleep and are willing to throw money at the problem could be the industry's salvation. This is, of course, dependent on the industry realizing that this "can't sleep" phenomenon is its only viable new market. Latex mattresses, high-line water beds, air mattresses, and all-natural mattresses are meeting the demands of Boomers who can't sleep and driving the average-unit sale prices through the roof. If you are in this business, go high or die.

Ironically, the bedding and mattress business is the bright spot in the overall furniture business. All other furniture categories are sucking wind and things will get worse. Conventional furniture sales are tied directly to home sales, and home sales are not going to recover anytime soon unless Generation Y enters the market very, very early. Boomers built houses for the last twenty years; now they would like to sell them and retire.

The problem is there aren't enough Generation Xers to buy them. We could see home sales in general stagnate for another ten years or more. (Probably more. Sorry.)

You can always tell when a consumer category is in trouble because it starts to offer no-payment, no-interest options. I heard one retailer offering no payments or interest until 2010. I could buy my furniture now and be dead by then. I guess my kids would have to pay for my furniture in that case. (I am waiting for the offer of no payments or interest ever. Then you would have my attention.)

The Future of Other Retail

What about big-box hardware stores like Home Depot? Cooked. Toast. The Boomer "Do-It-Yourselfer" is doing fewer and fewer of the big projects as he or she bumps up against retirement. Gen Xers don't have the critical mass to take up the slack, and Generation Y is too young. Immigrants don't own homes. Couple this with the drop in new home sales, and you have a troubling formula.

On the other hand, I am told that when the number of new homes being built begins to wane, kitchens and bathrooms step up to the plate. Remodeling kitchens and bathrooms is very profitable.

The eyewear industry is also taking a hit because of Generation X. Have you heard of presbyopia? It is an ophthalmic term that describes a vision condition referred to commonly as "old eyes." It generally manifests itself in men and women about forty to forty-five years of age and is probably the leading cause of routine vision issues. It's really no big deal, but it does require a trip to the ophthalmologist or optometrist. The symptoms of presbyopia are simple as well: You have difficulty reading and seeing clearly. This requires that you have your vision corrected by wearing glasses or contact lenses, and, if you have the means, even getting Lasik surgery.

Beginning in the early 1980s, optical chain stores opened like popcorn across the United States to meet the Boomers' rising demand for glasses and contact lenses. Many of these chains even incorporated in-store doctors of optometry into their business models to create a very convenient one-stop-shopping experience. As the Baby Boomer generation flooded the early eighties with forty-year-olds, the demand for glasses and contact lenses spiked and remained strong for twenty years. Now the demand for contact lenses and glasses is in a decline because our new presbyopes are the diminutive Generation Xers. You can look for this industry to remain in decline for another ten or fifteen years.

Remember the beer wars of the seventies and eighties? "Tastes great. Less filling." It was marketing genius. Where did they go? Did someone finally win? Was there a truce? No, sales declined. According to the National Highway Traffic Safety Administration, beer consumption fell by 10 percent from the early eighties to the year 2000. I bet you are wondering why.

You guessed it. The Baby Boomer generation exited the heavy beer-consuming age and grew up. As much as Generation X tried to consume at the Boomers' levels, it fell short because its critical mass is 11 percent less than the Baby Boomers'. *Are you starting to sense a pattern?*

Will the beer wars return? Yes, with a vengeance. Generation Y is honing its beer-drinking skills in colleges across the United States. It has taken beer drinking to a whole new level and it has the critical mass to outconsume even the Baby Boomers. I am sure records are falling everywhere.

Unfortunately, alcoholism will see a significant increase as well. And so will deaths on the highway, exacerbated by young drunk drivers. We lose about 45,000 people a year in traffic accidents. About one-third of them are young drivers. About one-sixth of them are young drunk drivers. New cars and motorcycles today can routinely reach speeds in excess of 100 miles an hour; make sure your kids know how to drive defensively and that they never drink and drive.

Avoiding Disaster

In conclusion, if you can understand the principles of shifting demography, you can forecast with uncanny accuracy what markets are growing and what markets are slowing. I really don't understand why more captains of industry and commerce don't use this data. Maybe it's because it would require them to think beyond the next quarterly report. Frankly, I am concerned that most businesses in the United States are operating without a plan. This is an invitation to disaster.

In addition, a lot of businesses simply do not want to hear bad news even if it can save them from derailing. I once received a call from a woman who was writing a story for an assisted-living association newsletter. She interviewed me for about ten minutes regarding the demographic forecast for the assisted-living market. She then stopped abruptly and said, "I can't write this." I asked her why, and she told me because it was bad news.

CHAPTER 23

The Great Y Ahead

More of Everything

There is an army of superconsumers headed right at us. Generation Y will be 100 million strong and its appetite for consumption is already 500 percent greater than Generation Y's parents. *Of massive marketing opportunities, Generation Y is the most massive in history.*

Born after 1985, with its birth peak in the year 1990, this market's boom has five years more than the twenty years allotted to other generations. Combined factors extend Generation Y's genesis through 2010. As masters of consumption, Gen Y understands outflow yet has no clue about income. What happened to those American icons—the lemonade stand and the paper route? Exactly what does "saving up for a bicycle" mean? There is no waiting; Gen Y wants it now. Where the money comes from has no significance. When this generation eventually leaves the fold and begins to forage for itself, it will make our world an interesting place because Generation Y will have never had to forage before.

Pregnancy postponement among the Boomers produced many older parents. Because a lot of first Boomer marriages fail, with second and third marriages commonplace, Gen Y kids can have four parents and at least eight grandparents. And these multiple parents/grandparents are showering these kids with presents, perhaps out of guilt to compensate them for the bad hand life has dealt them. This is going to be a handicap for Generation Y because its source of support will inevitably dry up and Gen Yers are going to face high unemployment and fierce competition as they enter the workforce.

The United States has a disproportionately high percentage of Generation Yers already. We have lots of Boomers and the Boomers had lots of kids. This will mean that Generation Y will have a very high unemployment rate as it enters the workforce because of the small footprint Generation X will leave behind. This is not all bad. It will precipitate a sea of young entrepreneurs who will start small businesses out of necessity to serve their own generation. This is what Boomers did in the seventies when they couldn't find work. The result is a very healthy economic engine that is great for our country.

> *"What happened to those American icons—the lemonade stand and the paper route? Exactly what does "saving up for a bicycle" mean? There is no waiting; Gen Y wants it now . . . . When this generation eventually leaves the fold and begins to forage for itself, it will make our world an interesting place because Generation Y will have never had to forage before."*

Opening a small business is a bit of a trick, though, and easily 90 percent of them fail in the first eighteen months. Some good information and training could cut the failure rate in half. There would be no shortage of interested support services to pay for this. Small business is the strength of our nation's economy, and Generation Y could reestablish small business like never before.

I forecast that small manufacturing companies will return to the United States for at least three big reasons. First, we have our own huge, homegrown, English-speaking, entry-level labor force; Generation Y. This labor force will be willing to work hard without high pay demands because of supply and demand. Everyone has to eat.

Second, when products are manufactured locally, they can be turned quickly—and manufactured profitably in small quantities. China cannot do this, period. Third, the price of shipping will continue to escalate unabated, and the time lag involved in overseas manufacturing and shipping will make China's products too slow to get to market.

Consider this. We are currently the only Western nation that had the good fortune to have a lot of kids. It is amazing to me how few intellectuals don't see a connection between children and the future. Generation Y is going to change our country.

Let's talk about green, for example. A huge part of Generation Y's legacy will be the Greening of America. We will all know our individual carbon-footprint numbers, just like we know our social security numbers. If we are polluters in work or play, we will have problems. In fact, we may not be able to work or play unless we clean up our acts. Can you imagine the pickup line, "So do you come here often, and what is your carbon-footprint number?"

Not all the news for the future is good. Crime will go up because of the sheer number of Gen Yers and the 2 percent factor (2 percent commit the crimes, 2 percent produce, the rest eat the food). In this case, 2 percent of 100 million means two million Gen Y crime committers. Crime will also go up because we'll have a unique combination of unemployed, undereducated young men with a huge appetite for consumption.

There's the additional problem of exponential progression. If two crime committers hook up with two other crime committers, the four will create the equivalent of six crime committers (i.e., 2 + 2 = 6). This is simple pack mentality. In a pack, people gain courage. When you have a criminal mind without courage, you don't have a crime. Crime is a communal activity.

Crime is also a hard way to make money. It's much easier to go to a job every day than it is to go out and commit crime. That's why crime committers tend to be fifteen- to thirty-year-old men. Crime is a young man's sport. Here's the good news: only 2 percent of the population commits the crime. And they grow out of it.

Consider, also, that the "2 percent factor" will contribute to an increase in the number of leaders, inventors, problem solvers, artists, philanthropists, scientists, and economists. Truly brilliant and splendid things will take place in our coming century.

And there are the rest who eat the food. That will be a market with 96 million buyers. Gen Y will suffer from 20 to 30 percent entry-level unemployment, making its members the perfect candidates for the armed forces.

Generation Y is now the largest generation in the history of the United States, bigger than the Baby Boomers. As described earlier, large populations like Generation Y that follow small populations like Generation X through the time continuum face unique challenges, especially when it comes to employment. Generation X cannot exit enough jobs as they age and move up the ladder to satisfy the job needs of Generation Y. The net is very high unemployment at the entry level.

Generation Y at this writing is twenty-four years old and under, peaked at age eighteen. Simply stated, we are going to have a lot of young men without work. As a result, the military will have all the young men they need to wage war, starting now and until further notice. So I guess you might say that if the United States was going to pick a time to stabilize the Middle East, especially Iran, it would be right now. I don't believe any of this is a coincidence.

CHAPTER 24

Marketing to Generation Y

I stopped my Volvo wagon at the top of our drive, got out to retrieve the mail, and got back in the car.

We get a lot of mail. My two daughters, ages thirteen and sixteen, chorused "Anything for me?" I thumbed through the stack, determined that they both had received letters with coupons from their favorite clothing retailer, and passed the envelopes to the backseat, where they were ripped open.

Then begins the drill: "Dad, can you take us to Bob's?" This is not a real question, because they know I'm trapped. How else will we save all the money reflected in the coupons? I am very familiar with the process because the retailer keeps these snail-mail incentives coming with train-schedule regularity.

There is a lesson here. Consider that my daughters are pretty typical. They have iPods, laptops, DVD players, and cell phones. They instant message, text message, voice message, and talk on their cells with a vengeance. They watch DVDs and listen to downloaded music. They do watch a little television, but the amount of time they spend in front of commercial broadcast/cable TV is declining significantly. They don't listen to broadcast radio or read newspapers at all.

So who cares? Marketers care. Why? Because they can't brand or, for that matter, even reach this new generation with any of the usual bag of advertising and marketing tricks. Gen Y has the potential to be the most consuming generation in the history of the United States—perhaps the world. It will be 100 million strong when the generation ends in 2010. It is consuming at 500 percent more than its parents, age for age, in adjusted dollars. The fact that marketers can't brand them borders on tragedy. In case you haven't heard, consumer brand-name preference is dropping like a stone. It's no wonder, considering that the largest and only emerging U.S. consumer market, Generation Y, is very difficult to reach with commercial, branding, and advertising messages.

This brings me back to the top of my driveway. Generation Y loves direct snail mail. I know this seems strange in a cyberage, but if you need to brand Gen Y and you are not using the U.S. Post Office, you are making a big mistake. Put some compelling coupons in a snail-mail offer and watch what happens.

How do you get a good mailing list? Work at it. You can buy a list for almost any market segment. Remember, however, it is one thing to buy a mailing list from a list vendor; it is quite another to maintain it and keep it current and clean. Don't get lazy with a mailing list, or the price of production and postage will kill you. If you are a retailer selling to members of Generation Y, don't let any of them leave your stores before you involve them in a carefully crafted retention program. For example, both of my daughters have Gap ID cards. Gap and Old Navy do a very good job of branding Generation Y.

Direct Mail's Magic 2 Percent

I can remember a very tense meeting in my office at KGA Advertising about seven years ago. The potential client wanted to understand the in and outs of direct marketing—in this case, direct mail. She owned a company that represented celebrities and public speakers who were typically hired to deliver keynote speeches for major organizations and corporations. The problem was that her sales had fallen off significantly and she was looking for a new way to promote her stable of speakers, especially some whom she had recently signed.

I knew she was a "just-the-facts" person, so I invited the owner of the direct-mail agency that KGA often partnered with to join me in the meeting. I did not want to get stumped on a question and look foolish. Direct mail is a tricky sell. I am well acquainted with broadcast and mass media, radio, television, newspaper, magazines, and billboards. Direct mail was in a class by itself, so I wanted backup.

"So what does all this cost and what do I get for my money?" she said. I explained that KGA would do the creative concept based on her description of the market and the actual targeted reader of the piece. We would then turn it over to the direct-mail experts, who would write the copy, design the component elements for printing, and put it in the envelopes. The direct-mail people would also be responsible for the selection of the appropriate mailing list and the actual mailing. The cost in this case was just under $10,000, all-inclusive, to mail about 5,000 pieces—about two dollars per mail piece. The price was not unusual for this type of narrow mailing, keeping in mind that the postage costs are fixed. There are only so many people in the United States who have the potential to hire public speakers. In a manner of speaking, this was definitely not mass marketing; this was focused, targeted marketing.

"And what exactly do you think my return will be?" she asked. I was about to answer when my direct-mail counterpart jumped in and said, "We don't know. Our responses historically have been running about 2 percent. However, your market is very esoteric and narrow, so this is anyone's guess—maybe one percent." I felt myself losing control of this presentation, but there was little I could do.

"Do you mean that 98 percent of this direct-mail product that I am paying for will be ignored or thrown away?" our stunned lady asked. Mr. Direct Mail looked at me as if to say, "Is this person really this unsophisticated (or stupid)?" He then turned to her and said, "What did you expect? We can't just mail to people who are ready to hire a public speaker. That mailing list does not exist." That was the last time I used him and the last time I saw her.

Mr. Direct Mail was a jerk, but he was right. A 2 percent return is considered a success in direct mail, which remains one of the most effective marketing tools for reaching Generation Y.

Snail Mail, Billboards, and the Internet

Billboards can be very effective marketing tools when used correctly. I love them, and I have built businesses with massive billboard campaigns. Yes, there will come a day when billboards will disappear. Billboards are also in the crosshairs of environmentalists who consider them a blight on America's landscape. For example, my wife was a member of the local chapter of the Garden Club of America. Her fellow members loved her, but I was a social leper because I posted commercial messages on billboards on Connecticut's beautiful highways.

Generation Y can be reached with creative billboard campaigns; the more creative, the better. Remember, billboards are not limited to two dimensions. I would routinely put huge three-dimensional objects on my boards to add to the drama.

For our bedding client, we had an enormous 3-D mattress built out of Styrofoam and secured to the face of the billboard. For our retail clothing and footwear client, we had a giant athletic shoe built and mounted on the board. People loved it and remembered the board. So build a mammoth iPod. Apple will help you.

Ok, so snail mail and billboards may sound like strange ways to reach Generation Y, but please take this advice seriously. I am very acquainted with good marketing and the value of early branding. Trust me, I have racked my brain to come up with a more sophisticated way of using media to brand Generation Y. These two mediums have left most of standard media behind—even, for now, the Internet.

Don't get me wrong. Internet marketing is the future. No question. However, the returns on investment (ROI) from Internet marketing are spotty at best. There are some real success stories, but most marketers don't have a clue what to do. That's the bad news. The good news is they will learn because they have to. Currently you cannot market to Generation Y without a dominant Internet component, period.

Here's an example. I once drove my kids to school while listening to National Public Radio. They were listening to their iPods. The reporter was interviewing a young male marketing expert about the enormous strides Google and others were making in reaching customers for their advertisers. Google essentially knows everything about everyone. It knows if you are a buyer or a looker. It has your buying history. It knows what you buy, when you buy it, how much you paid, and exactly how you paid for it. It knows what sites you visit and what you look at when you are there. It knows your buying patterns and how long you look before you buy. Google tailors the ads you get to see according to your tastes, habits, and history. You are truly an audience of one.

I know this is not breakthrough thinking, but Google is making it mainstream and very successful. Advertisers are flocking to it, and this is only the beginning. I have been in marketing and advertising for thirty-five years, but I am like an immigrant in the world of cyberadvertising. (I understand it, but I speak with a thick accent.) As I listened to this NPR interview, I realized that I really disliked this glib young marketing expert from an Internet agency with a goofy name as he described how my world was slipping away and his was taking over. But he was right. I thought immediately of my disastrous direct-mail meeting with the woman who wanted to reach only those people who were ready to hire a public speaker. My glib young cybermarketing expert, from Snake Bite or whatever the name of his agency was, could deliver this ready-to-buy market with ease.

My oldest daughter removed her earphones (or whatever you call them today) and asked, "What was that guy talking about?" I answered, "The end of my life as I knew it." She laughed. "What do you mean?" I explained that the world of marketing has changed, really changed, and turned the corner. Internet marketing until just recently was considered an untested novelty that produced marginal results. That would not be an accurate description now. The Internet is mainstream marketing. Radio, television, newspapers, magazines, and billboards are now anachronisms, relics waiting to be written about in history books. The newly rejuvenated beer wars and the battle between Coke and Pepsi will now have to be fought on a different battlefield. The mastery of the medium will be everything. It's a new day. "Really," she said. "But remember, Dad, people are still people and you know about people." Daughters are wonderful!

Hello Pepsi, Goodbye Coke: The End of the Cola War

Demography is all about change, and change is all about opportunity. Changing demography has an uncanny way of unseating incumbents; incumbent politicians, incumbent ideas, and incumbent products. Let's examine an incumbent product that is soon to be a victim of changing demography.

Coca-Cola has been the number-one-selling soft drink for generations—"The Real Thing" (whatever that is). What is Classic Coke anyway? It is a caramel-colored, flavored, carbonated water with enough corn syrup to float a boat. But so what, it sells. Coke enjoys the biggest market share of the soft drink market, with sales in the tens of billions of dollars. Coke's claim to fame was brilliant and effective marketing. You see, soft drinks are a demographically sensitive product because most soft drinks are consumed by teenage boys who can easily inhale a six-pack-plus per day. (Soft drinks are also great for the complexion and might have something to do with the nation's runaway child obesity issues. But that's another issue.)

Let's get back to the point. Astute marketers know that consumers age out of the sweet spot for their products, so they need to reach, market to, and brand younger consumers on an ongoing basis or their consumer bases will soon shrink. Coca-Cola employed this exact strategy for decades, winning new converts in the "cola wars" with the best TV and radio ads in the industry. Now along comes young Generation Y. You would think that Coke sales would go through the roof, right? Wrong. Why? Because the edge that Coke had over Pepsi—superior marketing—is ineffective with Generation Y. It barely watches television and it doesn't listen to commercial radio.

This is a dilemma of epic proportions on Madison Avenue, because marketing experts are unable to resolve this problem: They cannot find a way to effectively market to and brand Generation Y. As a result, Generation Y could easily become the most brand-disloyal generation in U.S. history.

Here is the real rub. Pepsi sales are up. Why? Think about it. What is Pepsi's signature product anyway? It is caramel-colored, flavored, carbonated water with enough corn syrup to float a boat. Yes, I know some people can tell the difference in taste tests, but Coke and Pepsi are really pretty much the same stuff. Strip Coke of its huge marketing advantage, and sales of the two products fairly displayed on supermarket shelves will force them to parity. I recently bought Pepsi stock.

CHAPTER 25

Case Study

No Leg to Stand On—A Levi's Footnote

Retail is detail. Retail can get into your blood. It takes a special disposition to work retail because the pay is not good, the work is difficult, and the hours are long. But some people like it. I was one of those people. I worked in a popular New England retail jean store called Bob's Surplus while I was in high school and for a few years after I got out of college. Bob was a brilliant merchant and I learned a great deal from him.

One of my most memorable lessons was the result of a conflict between Bob and the giant Levi Strauss and Company.

Levi's jeans sold like hotcakes and Levi Strauss insisted that its product be sold at the manufacturer's suggested retail price or we didn't get to sell them. This did not stop Bob from discounting Levi's jeans, because he operated, after all, a surplus store and he really didn't like to be told what to do. Levi's pulled its line after a shouting match on the selling floor between Bob and the Levi Strauss sales rep. I thought to myself, "It must be nice to be in such demand that you could demonstrate this kind of arrogance."

I don't know who mended the fences, but a few years later Levi's were back in Bob's Surplus. The law regarding a manufacturer's ability to dictate "manufacturer's suggested retail price" had changed, but Levi Strauss's arrogance had not. It had a new ploy. If you wanted to buy the jeans, you had to buy the other less salable products. I can remember the rep saying, "We can sell Levi's jeans in a drug store. We don't need you to sell our jeans." He would then calculate how much of the undesirable products Bob's ordered to determine how many Levi's jeans he would let Bob's have.

In Levi's defense, at the height of its popularity its product was like gold. Through the seventies, eighties, and early nineties, Levi Strauss's sales grew and so did Bob's Surplus, which is now called Bob's Stores. At one point at the height of Levi's popularity, they were selling for $75 a pair in Europe and the plan was to bring the United States price point as close to that level as possible. However, in the late 1990s a strange thing happened: Levi's jean sales went flat. Really flat.

My Free Lesson in Changing Demographics

In 1998, I got a call from a Levi Strauss marketing executive in San Francisco. As ad agency president, I directed everyone to be quiet. "I'm taking this call."

Levi's was the largest apparel manufacturer on the planet. Annual revenues were $8 billion. There was no "offshoring." It made its products domestically. At the time, I was the owner and president of KGA Advertising. At the time, we had handled all of Bob's Stores marketing for the last twenty years and had watched it grow from $10 million in sales to over $400 million. I had advised Bob's about our new research into shifting demography and how it was going to have to rethink its merchandise strategy, including the type of jeans that it would sell to the new, very young Generation Y market. Apparently, word had gotten back to Levi's that shifting demography just might be the reason its sales had gone south.

"I heard about your research in demographics. What does it say about us?" the Levi's executive asked me. As soon as I took the call, he told me Levi's wasn't looking for an ad agency and didn't intend to pay for the information. So I said, "All right. I'll just tell you the truth anyway. You're going to go out of business if you don't change."

There was a long silence. After he asked why, I said, "Because you've failed to see that the eighteen- to thirty-four-year-old market that is responsible for your success is not static." "Yeah, but that's the group that buys the most clothes," he countered. I gave him the math. "There are 11 percent fewer of those eighteen- to thirty-year-olds entering your market. The Baby Boomer generation that loved your product for the last twenty years can't fit in them anymore and has almost entirely exited its Levi's-buying years."

He asked me what I thought Levi's should do. I told him to totally refocus Levi's marketing. The Boomers were no longer prime jean customers. Generation X did not have the critical mass necessary to replicate the Boomers' sales volume. So the only answer was to put every marketing dollar it could into branding Generation Y, even though Generation Y at the time was peaked at only eight years old. He said they couldn't do that. "We're geared up for eighteen to thirty-four-year-olds and that's where we need to stay."

Unfortunately for Levi Strauss, this logic put them directly in the path of a market that would reduce its sales volume by 75 percent. The arrogance was gone.

I wondered, where are the executives getting their information? It seemed like they weren't doing their homework. They were certainly not gathering information from the simple, obvious arithmetic any U.S. Census chart would give them. This privately held business didn't go out of business. But they went from an $8 billion company to one with revenues of under $2 billion. Yes, Dockers (also made by Levi Strauss) have become part of a Boomer male uniform. In my opinion, Levi's got lucky on this.

Generation Y Will Lead the Fashion Parade

My advice to those who are currently running Levi Strauss would be to get ready for Generation Y. Generation Y's consumption of fashion will be huge and could launch Levi's sales to the levels of the old days. However, don't expect Generation Y to embrace the old standard Levi's styles automatically. It's not going to go down like that. This is a huge generation with very fragmented and individualistic ideas of what its members should look like. It's déjà vu all over again.

Remember the Boomer clothing styles of the late sixties and seventies: platform shoes, bell-bottom pants and jeans, Frye boots, sandals, carpenter's jeans, painter's pants, overalls, tie-dyed shirts, Indian shirts, acetate shirts, low-rise pants and jeans, leisure suits, hot pants, miniskirts, go-go boots, designer jeans, jogging shoes, sweat suits, leather jackets, and Levi's 501 prewashed jeans. These styles were precipitated by a generation that was finding its way. The Boomers are a huge generation and its impact on fashion and the clothing industry in general was profound.

As I mentioned in Chapter 22, humans are the most concerned about clothes when they are looking for mates, and the average age we get married in the United States is twenty-six. That's part of the reason the effect Generation Y has on the fashion industry should be nothing less than staggering.

An example of a company that speaks Generation Y's language is Converse. Converse takes its product—cool retro sneakers—directly to Generation Y's hangout, the Internet.

Generation Y kids love this product because they can customize their purchases to the nines on an extremely well-done website that is designed especially for them. They can create their own shoes exactly the way they want them, buy them online, and have them in no time. How about price? Who knows, it is not an issue. Generation Y does not find this process unusual, but it does find it very cool and is buying a lot of Converse sneakers. Marketers are going to have to realize that marketing to Generation Y must be done on Generation Y's terms. You could market to Generation X using Boomer ads. You definitely cannot market to Generation Y using Gen X concepts.

On a final note, Levi's advertising has always baffled me. The message was clear: You buy Levis' products and you get to have sex. The premise: Sex sells. The more sales declined, the more strident the ads became. Even their promotion of Dockers slacks to Boomer men promised sex. The harder the company tried, the less this strategy worked. Times change and "sex sells" is now an anachronism. May it rest, but not in peace.

> *"As soon as I took the call, he told me Levi's wasn't looking for an ad agency and didn't intend to pay for the information. So I said, 'All right. I'll just tell you the truth anyway. You're going to go out of business if you don't change.'"*

CHAPTER 26

Schools, Taxes, and the Future

I was shocked. I couldn't believe what my grandmother was saying. Could she really be this indifferent? She was, after all, talking about me and my education. It's not like I understood exactly what taxes were, but it was clear my grandmother did not want to pay them.

My mom, my brother, and I moved in with my grandmother on Long Island after my parents' divorce and the death of my grandfather in 1955. I was eight. I guess we all figured we would do better together by pooling our resources. The problem was, it was my grandmother's house and she never let us forget it.

Along with home ownership came property taxes and, as we all know, that's where the money comes from to fund education and new schools. It seemed that everywhere you looked, new schools were being built to accommodate a whole new crop of kids. The Baby Boom Generation was well on its way to being over 50 percent bigger than the Silent Generation born before it.

This meant schools, schools, and more schools. It also meant taxes, taxes, and more taxes. Grandmother's argument was sound. Her children were grown and didn't need these schools. Why did she have to pay to educate kids who weren't hers? Somehow my brother and I had fallen out of the equation. But I thought she made a good point.

My mother's rebuttal was interesting. She stated that paying school taxes was good for everyone. If we wanted a better country, we would just have to educate the kids. It sounded hollow, but I knew my mother wanted the best for me. Neither she nor my father had completed high school—a bitter fact that she regretted. She went on to say that if you didn't educate kids, they would become hoodlums. We would have to pay another way by being victims of crime. One point for mom.

My grandmother was not moved.

The Generational Battle over Taxes Is Correcting Itself

Taxes often are not fair. Taxes are the price we pay for civilization. I am involved in local government in the small town where I live in Connecticut. You quickly learn the things you can change and the things you can't.

There is very little you can do about property tax. About 80 percent of this tax funds education. The primary education expense is teacher's salaries. If you want to educate the kids, you need teachers, and you cannot put forty kids in a class, because education will not take place. So when the number of kids increases, as is the case with Generation Y—the biggest generation in the history of our nation—taxes will increase also.

Until just recently, very vocal members of the GI Generation were forcing endless referendums nationwide regarding school budgets in general and teachers' salaries in particular. The GI Generation was protesting because, like my grandmother, it resented paying for the education of someone else's kids. The members of the GI Generation for the most part lived on fixed incomes, had paid off their houses, and now saw that taxes were bigger than their mortgage payments used to be. You can empathize with their indignation. And to make matters worse, from their perspective, teachers were getting rich with salaries of $60,000 and $70,000 or more—and they didn't work in the summer.

Remarkably, this painful issue has been self-correcting. Quite simply, the GI Generation protestors are dying off and are now almost completely gone. You can't mandate referendums when you are dead. Members of the GI Generation leave their estates to their Boomer children who have kids in school.

When you have kids in school, you have a vested interest in education and seldom favor cutbacks.

There's more. The highly paid teachers the GI Generation loathed are Baby Boomers who have been in the system for decades. They are now making a dash for the door and retiring in droves. So who is replacing them? Generation Y kids fresh out of college. We are seeing the beginning of the wave right now.

Remember, the oldest members of Generation Y are young twentysomethings. There will be a sea of them coming out of college. This will naturally drive teachers' salaries down as the colleges crank out more Generation Y teachers than there are positions to fill.

We don't know yet exactly what Generation Y is going to bring to education, but you can be certain that changes are ahead. Green everything will be very big. Teacher lounges are going to be filled with an interesting nonhomogeneous, acrimonious population of emerging Generation Y, diminutive Generation X, and exiting, short-timer Baby Boomers. Generation Y will overwhelm teaching in the next ten years. The majority of the Boomer generation will have fled, and the defenseless Generation X will simply be outnumbered. Generation Y will be teaching Generation Y, just as Boomers taught Boomers in the seventies and early eighties.

To Build or Not To Build

The school-building boom extended well into the early 1980s before someone noticed there were fewer kids enrolling. By the end of the '80s, we had closed almost 20 percent of public schools in the United States because we didn't need them any longer. Many of these schools were then used as assisted-living facilities. Did anyone think that maybe, just maybe, the Baby Boom generation would have children and we might need those schools again? Apparently not, because here we are again, facing an enormous crop of school-age kids, the largest number our nation has ever seen. We are still seeing gross live births in the United States in excess of four million per year.

If only there was a way to predict the cyclical process of large and small generations, we could all save a lot of money. After all, who knows how many babies are going to be born? Don't you need a crystal ball? No. All you need is the U.S. Census. If you look at the live births for a twenty-year period, say 1925 to 1944, you'll see an inverted bell curve containing only 52.5 million people. The average number of children per couple during that time was a little over three. Do the math.

> *"Grandmother's argument was sound. Her children were grown and didn't need these schools. Why did she have to pay to educate kids who weren't hers? . . . I thought she made a good point."*

Fast forward to Generation X, born between 1965 and 1984, and you will discover another inverted bell curve containing about 69 million—or about 30 million couples times 2.3. There is an irony here, because the Silent Generation actually outperformed the touted GI Generation in making babies on a per-couple basis. Maybe it was because it had higher income per capita than its GI Generation counterparts or because there was a reduction in infant mortality.

My point is, you can predict when a generation will be the market for school buildings. And you can predict when it will be the market for any product or service throughout its life cycle. I don't know why this is such an elusive concept.

Because we have not been paying attention to generational cycles, there is one very significant difference in conditions surrounding Generation Y as opposed to its Baby Boomer parents when it comes to public education: We the people, the taxpayers of this great country, are not building new schools for Generation Y at the rate we did for Baby Boomers. Gen Y will just have to make do with old, substandard buildings, fewer teachers, larger classes, and, in general, a lesser education than their parents. This will cause the rich to pull their kids out of public schools and put them in private schools, further exacerbating the situation.

If there is a bright spot in public education right now, it would have to be the change in the nation's technical secondary schools. There was a time not that long ago when the technical schools were filled with the kids who were castoffs from the mainstream high schools—the recalcitrant. Well, the paradigm has shifted and shifted dramatically.

Because Generation X for the most part did not elect to become tradespeople, the United States has an acute shortage of what we used to call "blue-collar" trained technicians. So, as the Boomer tradespeople retire, the demand for technical labor has increased geometrically. The technical schools in the United States have stepped up to the plate, dramatically upped their standards, and are beginning to graduate blue-ribbon crops of skilled labor, young entrepreneurs, and business owners. Yes!

Here's one final thought related to public education. The tragedy at Columbine High School in Colorado was a wake-up call for all parents and teachers worldwide. A similar heartbreak occurred in a Finland high school in November 2007. The unconscionable is now becoming too common. A close examination of some video games provides an insight into the near reality of the violence-filled cyberworld a lot of kids live in. In the video games, the victims get up to play again. In real life they don't. I am very concerned that there are more and more troubled young people who cannot tell the difference.

I put my kids in private school. I remember what my mother said to my grandmother . . . especially the hoodlum part.

> *"I remember what my mother said to my grandmother . . . especially the hoodlum part."*

CHAPTER 27

Generation Y's Leading Legacy

It is easy being green!

Generation Y could be the first generation in the world to leave the earth a better place than they found it. If you don't think the green concept is catching on, then you must live in a closet. It is everywhere, and the undercurrent is more like a riptide. It has corporations shaking in their boots and scrambling for a green story to tell. Corporations used to fear hostile takeovers. Now they fear environmentalists and the attendant bad press.

Generation Y takes being green seriously, very seriously. *By 2010, Generation Y (born 1985 to 2010) will be 100 million people strong. It will be the single biggest market the United States has ever known.* When Generation Y speaks, you better listen, and Generation Y will be speaking about being *green.*

In the late 1960s and early 1970s, the Baby Boomers began to reorder American culture. They changed everything from our music and art to the cars that we drive. Baby Boomers really love change. Boomers are now changing the way we retire. And when their time is up, they will change the way we die. So if you are in the funeral business, start thinking up cool ways to check out.

Two of the most redeeming cultural changes that the Boomers will leave as a legacy are tolerance and diversity. Boomers taught us to be tolerant of others even if they were different, if they looked different, or thought different. It was okay.

Boomers, in general, hate hypocrisy and bigotry. They considered their parents to be both, thus the divide that came to be called the "Generation Gap." Today our culture is infinitely more tolerant and diverse than it was forty years ago, when the GI Generation ran things. Need proof? In 2008, *both* a woman and an African American male were leading candidates to be President of the United States. This is a serious change. However, I think the scope and degree of change precipitated by the Boomers will wax pale compared to what's in store from Generation Y.

The Generation Y Society

When I was in high school and college I had a difficult time meeting girls. I don't know why, but I always felt awkward just walking up to girls whom I didn't know and engaging them in conversation. Some guys were good at it, but not me. Most of the time, I just admired them from a distance. My college roommate, Chuck Jamieson, who was from Hawaii, was a natural. He could approach any girl any time, and in no time Chuck and the girl would be old friends. I stuck close to Chuck, but the skill did not rub off. We would practice opening lines like, "Don't I know you?" or, "So, are you from around here?" or, "Do you come here often?" But nothing ever really worked for me. I met my wife by asking her boss to send her to the vending machines at work when I just happened to be there, and even that was awkward.

Remember, the Boomer's signature pick-up line was "What's your (astrological) sign?" Well, get ready for the latest pick-up line, this time from Generation Y: "So, what's your carbon-footprint number?" Leave it to Generation Y to make meeting the opposite sex a green issue. Leave it to Generation Y to make everything people do a green issue.

For example, imagine a conversation between two Generation Y teenage girls.

First girl: "You ok? Did you and Tanner break up?"

Second girl: "I knew it couldn't last. He just pretended to care about having a low number. I told him a low carbon-footprint number is important to me. I thought he cared. Then I find out that he actually removed the catalytic converter from his Honda to make it go faster. Do you know what that does to his number and our relationship?"

The 600-Pound Green Gorilla

Generation Y is a giant emerging market that is bigger than the Baby Boomer generation and the market it created. If you can accept that the way you learn to consume will ultimately determine the way you consume as you age and gain earning power, then you will have to agree that Generation Y will be a 600-pound gorilla that will send consumer spending into the stratosphere. This is very good news for the U.S. economy and our trading partners. However, selling to this generation is not going to be a given just because your company has a cool product or service.

Generation Y will look deeper into who you are and want to know about your company policies on recycling, environmental responsibility, company initiatives, pollution history, and human rights. Ultimately, one of the biggest casualties of Generation Y's market dominance will be China and big-box retailers like Wal-Mart. If your sole goal is low price, you will need to rethink your Generation Y strategy. In addition to Generation Y's penchant for the latest hot fashion, which big boxes will have difficulty delivering anyway, it will make demands on retailers regarding the fair treatment of the labor that produced the clothing. What are Wal-Mart and China going to do with that one?

Baby Boomers really do not care where products are made, who made them, under what conditions, how they were made, or what the expense is to the environment. If you want to sell to a Baby Boomer, you really only need to remember three Boomer conditions for business: make my life easy, save me some time, and don't rip me off. Selling to Generation Y will be far more complex and infinitely more green and humanitarian.

When our advertising agency, KGA, was about five years old, I hired an attorney to sift through the huge stack of state and federal advertising and marketing regulations that governed the industry. When combined, the stack of regulations was about a foot tall and appeared overwhelming. I did not want to lose any clients over a mistake or oversight, and I certainly didn't want to end up in court. I remember thinking as the attorney walked out of our office with the regulations under his arm: What is this going to cost and how long is his report going to be?

Well, the day came a couple of weeks later when the attorney returned with the stack of regulations and ceremoniously dropped them with a crash in the center of the conference table where we all had assembled. He then stated that he had considered writing a long report but that avoiding conflict with the state and federal regulations could be summed up in one sentence. "One sentence?" I asked incredulously. "Yes," he said,

"One sentence: *Thou shalt tell the truth!*" I liked that report. It was simple, actionable, and very effective. We never had a problem with the regulations after that.

My advice to companies that are gearing up for Generation Y business is simple: *Have fun and tell the truth.* Produce, sell a quality product or service in a responsible environment, and let Generation Y know what you're doing in a cool way. Generation Y will beat a path to your door. I saw a cool example in my daughter's March 2008 *Teen Vogue* magazine. The headline on the ad reads, "If everyone who reads this magazine wears a pair of ecoSNEAKS, about 284,904 car tires will avoid the landfills." The company is called Simple (www.simpleshoes.com). The Paul Mitchell (www.PaulMitchell.com) ads in the same magazine are very aggressive as well, with the lines "Giving Back is the New Black," and "Bang to a Different Beat. Plant a Tree and Keep Our Planet Cool." However, don't think you can just say it. You must do it.

Generation Y's green influence will spread north into Generation X, and even slip a little bit into the Boomer generation. I see Boomer men at our town's transfer station begrudgingly separating their recyclables and tossing them into the designated dumpster. Generation X finds recycling more natural, but it is definitely a cultural shift that will be credited to Generation Y. Generation Y will make green mandatory and mainstream.

I pity companies that don't pay attention to green issues. The same goes for companies that pretend to care and devote token initiatives to real problems. This is called "green washing." This complacency could cost them their businesses. The computer industry is rife with these selfish outlaws. Take linear tape open (LTO) backup data cartridges as an example. There are 80 million of these cartridges in the United States, with no large-scale plan to recycle them even though the technology exists to erase them and reuse them. Instead, they are incinerated and put in landfills because the two major manufacturers of LTO cartridges, Imation and Fujifilm, don't want to jeopardize the sales of new products. This kind of blatant corporate selfishness and arrogance will eventually come back and bite both of these shortsighted organizations in the butt.

Just remember that the green movement is not temporary. You need to develop a comprehensive, holistic, and, above all, flexible green policy and then live by it. It's here to stay, so don't play games with it or you could really lose. You don't want GreenPeace to park a boat in front of your headquarters.

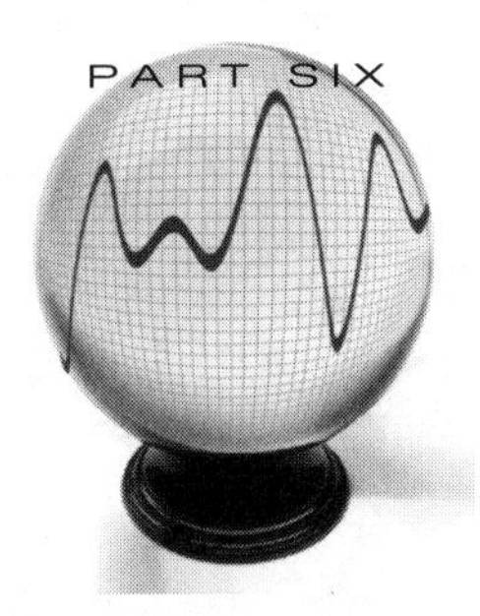

The Generation Impact of Social Issues

CHAPTER 28

The Bigotry Is Almost Gone—A Boomer's Perspective

In 1955, Sammy Davis, Jr. impulsively jumped into a swimming pool at the Las Vegas Strip hotel where he was headlining but not allowed to stay. He was hot. The water was cool. He was refreshed.

The hotel drained the pool. *Yes, that's right—drained the pool!*

Sammy had to stay at a hotel that catered to Negroes on the outskirts of town. He was not even allowed to gamble in the casinos. No Negroes allowed! If he wanted to buy some new clothes, he had better guess right on the size because Negroes were not allowed to try on new clothes. If they tried them on, they had to buy them. (I wonder what people thought we would catch from them.)

In 1966, my African American fraternity brother from high school, Freddy Hickson, and I were fooling around wrestling until we both broke into a sweat. When we broke free I looked down at my drenched clothing and he said, "Don't worry Ken, it doesn't rub off." He was referring to the color of his skin. It was a strange comment that really caught me off guard. He knew the comment hit its mark, and so did I. Is that what people feared?

On December 1, 1955, a forty-two-year-old black woman was arrested for disorderly conduct while riding a city bus in the deep South. She was in violation of a Montgomery, Alabama, municipal law that required "colored people" to ride in the back of the bus. She was sitting in the first row of seats designated for colored passengers. When a group of white men boarded, Jimmy Blake, the bus driver, ordered her to give up her seat and move farther back in the bus. Can you imagine the indignation, pent-up hostility, and frustration? She was already sitting in the colored section. She was already deferring to the condescending, demeaning city ordinance that defined her second-class citizenship. Somehow it wasn't enough. She was asked to stoop lower. She refused. The rest is history. Her name was Rosa Parks.

I like to tell people I was for women's rights in the '60s, but I can't prove it. I do know I treated women differently than my jock friends did. I hated their locker-room stories. You did things to women and then you told the guys about it. It's like women weren't real people. If they weren't real people, then there was no obligation to treat them as equals, and my friends didn't. I did. I was the odd man out and I didn't care.

"It's like women weren't real people. If they weren't real people, then there was no obligation to treat them as equals, and my friends didn't. I did. I was the odd man out and I didn't care."

Well, maybe I cared a little bit. A guy likes to be one of the guys. But as president of the elite club, Sigma Chi, in my senior year, I lobbied heavily for inducting the first Jew and the first African American in the club's history. It was a wonderful victory. (Danny Shapiro referred to himself as the only "Sigma Kike.")

Nigger, Wop, Kraut, Kike, Frog, Limey, Mick, Pole, Swede, Spic, Chink, Nip, Gook, Gypsy, Camel Driver, Old Lady, and Dumb Broad were all acceptable names for human beings in my household. You didn't negotiate with people, you "Jewed them down." If you paid too much, you were "Gypped." The words *dumb* and *typical* could be added for effect and precede any name. One of my clearest memories as a kid was hearing about the "typical woman driver." This "dumb broad" was not to be trusted behind the wheel. I never felt entirely safe with my mother driving and always checked out other cars in traffic to see if any "typical women drivers" were putting us in jeopardy. It was no way to live.

When it came time to date, the mandate was clear. "You bring home a white girl and not just any white girl, a white girl like us." I often wondered what would happen if I brought an African American girl home. My parents would have been stunned and in need of emergency medical help. An Italian girl maybe, but not an African American girl, not a Jewish girl, and not an Asian girl, or you are out the door. A mixed marriage like that of Sammy Davis, Jr. and May Britt was a spectacle in the early sixties.

In WWII, many white U.S. soldiers would not fight side-by-side with African American U.S. soldiers. They fought separately. "You can't trust Niggers," was their refrain. College basketball coaches in the South would pull their players off the floor rather than compete against African American players.

What were people thinking? Why did so many of our parents teach us prejudice? Why was this ok?

How Much Things Have Changed

In the late 1960s, young people in the United States began to create a counterculture. One of the first things to go was prejudice. It was stupid and obviously wrong. Bob Dylan sang songs about it. Boomers embraced it—and they never let go. Sweeping change took place both legislatively and culturally.

When she was in grade school, my daughter Hayley spoke of her new friend Chelsea often enough to make her part of our daily conversation, even though my wife and I had never met her. Chelsea and her family had just moved to town. It was always, "Chelsea did this" and "Chelsea did that." "Chelsea got an A on her paper." "Chelsea and I are partners on the science project." We would ask questions about Chelsea, and our daughter would answer within the context of her day. So it was with a degree of anticipation that that we looked forward to meeting her new friend at a concert. "Chelsea will be sitting three people away from me to my left," said Hayley.

We arrived and sat down in the auditorium as the kids filed in to take their places. The lights dimmed and the concert began. I counted three kids to Hayley's left and saw Chelsea. She was African American. We don't have a very diverse town. Our African American population might be twenty or thirty people out of several thousand. My daughter never mentioned anything about Chelsea's race (it never even occurred to her) and we never asked. I leaned over to my wife and said, "Chelsea is African American." It was obvious that my wife already knew, because I could see the tears of pride welling up in her eyes. We had taught our kids to ignore skin color, but we didn't expect them not to see it at all. I later asked Hayley why she didn't tell us that Chelsea was African American. She just innocently shrugged her shoulders and said she didn't know.

The Boomers began working to change American culture. Generation X, too, made great strides toward openness and diversity. People were accepted regardless of race, creed, religion, or sexual orientation. Generation Y, represented by my daughter, Hayley, has simply blown the doors off the old bigotry. Its members don't even notice or mention that their new friends are African American.

In the late sixties, the old guard took its bigoted thinking underground. It changed on the surface, but many people did not really change in their hearts. They did the right thing publicly. But in secret, they were unchanged. They expressed their bigotry in more subtle ways.

Remember the Golden Rule: He who has the gold, rules. The GI Generation still has a lot of the gold. But most of that generation is already dead. The generation's remnants still control a significant part of the nation's personal wealth. This personal wealth comes with political power and board seats.

So why do you think there are so few women and minority C-level executives? Is it because they are unqualified? Of course not! It's because there has been a lingering bigotry at work. But, thankfully, that bigotry is almost gone. Like rays of light, leaking through the darkness here and there, certain change is coming.

The next possessor of the gold is the Boomer, and the Boomer is all about change. Some of this change is bad. We discarded some important virtues of the GI Generation, which was long on integrity ("My word is my bond"). Boomers are short on integrity, vividly reflected in our 50 percent marriage-failure rate. "Till death do us part or unless we change our minds," and "I meant it when I said it," could cripple our ability to do business.

But some of the change we're bringing is very good. The Boomer understands diversity. We will see an end to the Glass

Ceiling. The Boomer doesn't care what color you are, so minorities will suddenly find themselves with more freedom and opportunities than they can consume. There will be no need to play the race card. Dylan sang, "The times they are a-changin'," and it turns out he was right.

And the parade moves on.

> *"Like rays of light, leaking through the darkness here and there, certain change is coming."*

Clearly as a nation we have made some progress. There are many African Americans enjoying the American dream, but their numbers still are too few. I often contrast Condoleezza Rice with Rosa Parks to demonstrate our nation's progress in diversity. There aren't enough of these contrasts. I do, however, believe that we will see more and more diversity and less bigotry as the Baby Boomers take their positions of power and board seats. The net effect of this change will be gradual but sure.

And as Generation X and then, in such massive numbers, Generation Y, take their place at the head of the table, bigotry should be a distant memory and diversity should rule the day. That is real progress.

CHAPTER 29

Coming to America
Melting Into the World's Melting Pot

I don't know what set off the language change, but when we least expected it, my mother would make her point in German. This usually happened when she was excited, angry, or both. The funny part about it was that it came out of nowhere and would even be a surprise to her.

"Sitz dich hin!" meant, "Sit down! Now!" When she told you that you had a "mutz kopf," it was a warning to lose the pouty lip and stop feeling sorry for yourself. We didn't say "God bless you" after someone sneezed. We said, "Gesundheit." When mother wanted to speed things along, she would say, "Schnell, schnell." The irony was that my mom wasn't fluent in German and never actually spoke the language.

My parents were not German immigrants. They were born in Queens, New York. My grandparents and great-grandparents were not German immigrants. They were born here in the United States. It was my great-great-grandparents who came here in the 1840s and 1850s. They were the immigrants. They were at the start of the flood of German immigration extending through 1925. These German immigrants would number more than those coming from any other single country—even to this day. There are currently more than 60 million people in the U.S. of German descent.

Early on, like many other nationalities, the Germans settled into lower-Manhattan neighborhoods that provided protection and a cultural cocoon. German immigrant men married German immigrant women. They spoke German as a first language and struggled with English only by necessity. Kids spoke German at home and learned English in school. Keep in mind that not all kids went to public school, because that concept was relatively new until the early 1900s. Even then, attending school was spotty at best. So "language isolation" prevailed and thus ensured an undiluted German culture.

In a historic move, these immigrant communities pulled up stakes and crossed the East River. They settled in rural Brooklyn and Queens in the early 1900s. The geography changed, but little else did. Germans still married Germans.

Second- and third-generation immigrants still spoke German fluently.

They remained an autonomous culture—and an autonomous market. They bought and ate German-style food, enjoyed German music, and drank German-style beer. They worked at familiar German crafts. Even though my parents were third-generation Americans, they found it convenient to marry within the same culture in 1936. That's almost 100 years after the initial immigration.

That nationality has now dissolved into the melting pot. It's gone. It's a part of the overall American culture. Germans came to the United States because they wanted what Americans had. They wanted opportunity. Now they have it and they are an indiscernible part of it.

Fast forward to the twenty-first century. We hear a popular concern that Asian and Latino immigrants are not relinquishing their cultural identities fast enough to suit the "real Americans." I wonder how many of those critics have German, Polish, French, and Italian names? How soon we forget who we are. We're a nation of immigrants! It's the newly arrived versus the not so newly arrived.

Let's consider the Latinos. They make up by far the lion's share of critical mass in new U.S. immigrants. Can we blame them for coming? We're close by. Some can walk here. The contrast between their home countries and the United States is so marked they often risk their lives and pay enormous sums of money to get here. We should be flattered. And we should be grateful for what they add to our way of life. Latinos have a strong sense of family and an excellent work ethic. Few would disagree that this is exactly what we need.

I attended college in Southern California and lived there for a while after college before moving back to New England. One of the things that impressed me about the Latino culture was that on any given Sunday you could go into a Denny's restaurant and see large, well-dressed extended Latino families sitting together with tables pushed together. It was obvious that they had attended church services together and now they were enjoying a family time that included everyone from the great-grandparents to the newborns. They were happy people who understood what a family is. They stuck together and cared for each other. You just knew that the elderly were cared for in a family member's home, because that was their way. In contrast, my family put elderly family members in assisted-living facilities. The Latino immigrants had a real work ethic, strong family bonds, and a moral compass instilled by their Catholic faith.

The Latino Market

The fluctuation of the birthrate has a critical impact on business. But my reference point so far has been to U.S. births—the number of immigrants born here is zero.

Immigrants have not yet affected generational buying patterns, because the bulk of our new immigrants have not even been here twenty years. After all, the United States is the great melting pot, but it takes a while to melt into the stew. In our case as Germans, it took over 100 years. Melting is slow, but it is sure. Until then, immigrant cultures remain an influential—but very distinct—market force of their own.

Those peaks and valleys of generational buying behaviors affecting business remain intact for the time being. For example, Latino immigration has completely filled in the numbers deficit in U.S. population currently occupied by Generation X (born between 1965 and 1984) bringing the total number of people in the Generation X age group to 80 million, and then some, making this group as large as the Boomers (born between 1945 and 1964). Yet, culturally, these immigrants are a "layer" that is separate from native-born Gen Xers. The layer of immigrants adds numbers to each generation but has not culturally permeated the generational mass beneath it. The layer does not significantly affect the purchasing preferences of its corresponding age group. That will come later.

Meanwhile, Latino immigrants have their own culture, their own market, their own clothes, their own cars, their own food, their own music, their own language, and—when they become citizens—their own vote.

The Latino market is growing along with Latino spending power. There are two significant reasons for this. The first reason is that the most bigoted part of our population, the GI Generation (now eighty-five plus), is almost completely gone. This removes cultural barriers to career advancement. The second reason is a critical shortage of managers and skilled labor in the Generation X age bracket of twenty-four to forty-three. This age bracket is exactly that of the Latino immigrants, because that's where the void in our labor market existed and that's the main reason they came here in the first place. It is a simple case of supply and demand. Commerce needs managers. The best and the brightest of the Latino immigrants are in the right place at the right time. Latinos will advance in their careers and make more money. This also bodes well for the housing market. Latinos, many of whom were victims of the subprime debacle, will be able to qualify legitimately for mainstream mortgages.

The Latino consumer market is worth several hundred billion dollars and should be attractive to marketers willing to specialize in this remarkable subcategory. If you are a marketer and you choose to pursue the Latino market, let me give you a very valuable piece of advice. There are two ways to market to Latinos. One is to direct your standard marketing message to them in English and simply place the ads in media directed to them. Many Latinos actually prefer this because this is after all their country, too, and English is spoken here. The second way to market to Latinos is to prepare a special message just for them and present it in Spanish.

What you want to avoid like the plague is translating your standard English marketing message into Spanish. It doesn't survive the translation and you *will* offend them. For example, the *Miami Herald* tried translating its paper into Spanish to reach the vast Cuban population in south Florida. The

Cubans found it insulting and rejected it wholesale. Then the Miami Herald began publishing *El Nuevo Herald.* The Cubans embraced it.

The food industry (supermarkets) has also been successful in marketing to the Latino populations by using Latino media. A U.S. Food Marketing Institute report released in 2005 stated that Hispanics/Latinos fork over an average $133 a week on groceries, compared to only $92.50 by everyone else. They also shop more often by a factor of two, according to the study. That's 100 percent more shopping. Think about it. In the Latino culture, buying fresh is very important because in the countries where they (or their parents) come from, open-air markets are common. As the Latino market grows, supermarket chains that don't seize on this "fresh" concept when marketing to Latinos are missing a huge opportunity. Latinos all by themselves could reverse the trend of restaurant sales outpacing those of the supermarkets. Do the math: Latino expenditures per week are 44 percent larger than everyone else's. That is a significant difference.

I like the Latino market because it has nowhere to go but up. And, believe me, it will go up. Half the 4 million plus babies born in the United States in 2007 were Latino. Without the Latino contribution to fertility in the United States, we simply would not be at replacement level; it would be very likely the United States would not be the United States in fifty years. So please lose the ridiculous anti-immigrant rhetoric. In fact, kiss a Latino on the lips and thank him or her for being here.

The Anti-Immigration Debate

One of the ironies of the anti-immigrant rhetoric is that, eventually, Latino immigration will stop all by itself. These immigrants did not come to the United States for political asylum or religious freedom. They came here to work because there was work. The immigration/border issue will be resolved in less than five years without any help from vigilantes, rabid politicians, and needless legislation. The current immigration situation in the United States is precipitated by uneven demography.

For instance, beginning in 1965, the birthrate began to drop, bottomed out in the mid-seventies and recovered in the mid-eighties. The net result was a deficit of about nine million people over a twenty-year period. Remember all the public school closings in the seventies and early eighties? This is why. When this population entered the workforce, lower-paying, undesirable jobs went begging. The Latino immigrants came and took those jobs. They did not come here to take jobs away from anyone. They just came for the jobs that were unfilled. Job vacancies suck in immigrants like a huge vacuum cleaner. It's a natural economic phenomenon.

The same trend happened in Europe involving North African immigrants. Europe is now heavily populated with young Muslims having huge families. Overall, Europe's indigenous birthrate remains well below replacement level, essentially guaranteeing that Europe will not be Europe in fifty years. Unlike Europe, the U.S. birthrate began to climb in 1985 and has never looked back, resulting in a crop of kids currently under twenty-four that outnumber the Baby Boomers. This is the new labor force for entry-level, low-paying jobs—homegrown and in overwhelming abundance.

If there are no jobs, there will be no immigration. Word gets around fast. Many of the illegal Latinos will go home. They will have to because there won't be any work for them. We are going to look pretty foolish with these big fences along our southern borders. We're going to have to take them down to let the immigrants out. Ironically, with the rapid economic advances taking place in Mexico, some of our surplus members of Generation Y will go there to find work. (We can sell the Mexicans our fences.)

If you need proof on the upcoming flight of immigrants, take a look at the immigration data for the 1930s depression economy. In the 1920s, European immigrants poured into the United States at the rate of about 1 million per year. In the 1930s, that number dropped to near zero without any legislation. In this case, a little more history and math would serve our leaders well.

In summary, just as immigrants have always done for our nation, Latinos, Asians, and other immigrants add to our immense strength and the rich diversity of our fabric. Immigrant cultures will be assimilated, and just as in the past 300 years, our lives are better for it. And when I get impatient I still tell my children to "Sitz dich hin!"

C H A P T E R 30

Macro and Micro Conclusions

I was recently keynote speaker for an annual event sponsored by the Connecticut Department of Labor. I was scheduled to go on after lunch, but I arrived a couple hours early because I always like to get a lay of the land and check out the audience. Prior to my presentation to the entire group, I sat in on a breakout session given by the Bureau of Labor Statistics. The presenter was a Ph.D. who was younger, thinner, and better looking than me. That would be ok by itself, but according to the program I had just been handed, he was speaking on the exact same topic I was. It said "The Demography of the United States Labor Force." That's my topic. Didn't anyone check? Wouldn't this be redundant?

This guy and his staff—yes, staff—are going to make a fool of me, I thought. His research resources are a thousand times better than mine. He is a Ph.D. I have a B.A. from a blue-collar university in California. I could feel the "flop sweat" starting already. ("Flop sweat" is a phrase used by stand-up comedians to describe the perspiration that turns on like a faucet when no one laughs at your jokes.) I wondered if I had been set up by some secret enemy who wanted to silence me forever. This was awful.

His presentation started very well. He even warmed up the group with a couple of jokes. Believe me, people who work in this environment are starved for humor. Our Ph.D. speaker was a well-respected and high-ranking Bureau of Labor Statistics official. He reviewed more than 100 slides covering extensive research on the very subject I was going to speak about. I have to admit that initially I wondered why he wasn't the keynote. I am sure he was very smart, but he very quickly displayed an ignorance of and indifference to his audience. If he really wanted to inform us, he failed. If he wanted to impress us, he succeeded.

I felt dwarfed and overwhelmed by his expertise. That is, until the end of his presentation. I looked around the room and realized that I was just one of sixty dwarfed and overwhelmed people attending this session.

What could we collectively or individually conclude from such extensive research shared by this powerful and learned man? Nothing; our brains were fried. Don't get me wrong. He undoubtedly had the correct information. It's just that his micro approach had necessitated breaking the information into so many pieces and viewing it from so many angles that you could barely recognize it. Kind of like trying to understand a cow by examining 100 cuts of meat. It wasn't even a forest-from-the-trees issue. This guy got into the DNA. And 100 slides in less than one hour—what was he thinking?

The real irony here was not our corporate intellectual stupor, but the fact that the Ph.D. knew he left us all behind early in the presentation, and he had no problem with that. I had the sense he had given this presentation many times before. He had fun. We were in pain. Why was he even wasting his time with the proletariat?

I couldn't believe that he only allowed five minutes for questions, but as it turned out the time was quite adequate. There were none. We all needed counseling.

An hour later, I spoke for an hour on the same subject. I used two slides: U.S. motorcycle sales and live births in the United States. Call me Mr. Macro. I drew countless real-life, commonsense conclusions and fielded more questions than I had time to answer. The people were starved for information they could understand and use. That is the point.

You can't make informed decisions at any level if you are not informed; and you can't be informed if the information is locked in a complicated, obscure, perplexing communications system suitable only for a statistician. There is universal concern about power and wealth being in the hands of fewer and fewer people. The dissemination of power and wealth begins with the dissemination of good information that the average person can understand and use.

Now that you are familiar with my writing style, you know that I am very macro and that I will err on the side of simplicity. I hate information people cannot understand or use, no matter how well researched or valid it is. I believe that information should solve mysteries, not create them. I have therefore reduced my demographic information into easy-to-understand corollaries that lean toward broad generalizations. These generalizations are very valid and rife with common sense. There will, of course, be seemingly contradictory anomalies, but please ignore them—you won't sacrifice an accurate big picture.

I learned a new acronym recently: EGO. It stands for "Eyes Glassed Over." It is another way of saying bored, disinterested, or simply, "I don't get it." My eyes used to glass over in high school and even in college. It is a painful experience. Your body wants to shut down at the very time you want it to be alert so you can assimilate new information. I always thought it was me—that I lacked comprehension skills or maybe even had Attention Deficit Disorder (ADD). My ADD was selective, however, especially when it came to teachers and professors. Why did I love some classes and dread others? I came to the conclusion that my instructors fell neatly into two categories:

those who wanted to impress me with what they knew, and those who wanted me to know what they knew. The latter were teachers—real teachers.

I'm not suggesting that U.S. Census data and the principles of shifting demography that make up generational marketing will ultimately give us the answer to world peace. I am saying that the principles put forth in this book, when understood, will go a long way to helping everyday people comprehend the world around them from a profound commonsense perspective.

APPENDIX A
The Older Generations

There are five distinct generations alive in the United States today. The bulk of this book deals with the last three of these, the Baby Boomers, Generation X, and the Echo Boomers, or Gen Y. As explained in this book, only two of these generations—the Boomers and Gen Y—can yield worthwhile returns on a marketer's investment because they follow small generations and therefore spawn expanding markets. Small generations that follow large ones get dwarfed by them. The Silent Generation, as with Generation X later, lives in the wake of an enormous generation, the GI Generation.

Fast Facts About the GI Generation:

- From 1905 to 1924, there were 56.6 million live births in the United States. The GI Generation reached close to 70 million strong when you factor in European immigration. There are only about 5 million hearty souls left alive at this writing.

- The GI Generation experienced the Great Depression and fought hard in World War II.

- They were very patriotic and strong supporters of the American way.
- They held their families together, made commitments, and kept promises.
- Their word was their bond.
- This generation had a slew of kids—the Baby Boomers.
- They were savers and frugal spenders who left $7 to $10 trillion dollars to their Boomer kids.
- They moved out of the cities into the suburbs.
- They drove big American and European cars. They refused to drive Japanese cars.
- They embraced blue-collar work.
- They liked to drink.
- They held bigoted attitudes with serious prejudice against anyone unlike themselves.
- Overall, the GI Generation was a noble generation willing to sacrifice.

MARKETING TO THE GI GENERATION

I don't think so. If they have lived this long, someone is caring for their needs. However, as a political force and contributor, this generation will be missed dearly by the Republican Party.

Without this generation, we (the United States) would be speaking German or Japanese.

Fast Facts about the Silent Generation

- The Silent Generation was born from 1925 to 1944, with a total of 52.5 million live births.
- This was the smallest generation of the last 100 years.
- They were unaffected by immigration because of the Great Depression and World War II.
- The Silent Generation followed meekly in the shadow of the GI Generation.
- They adopted the GI Generation's art, music, clothing, and overall culture.
- They lived modestly and saved their money.
- They were civic-minded.
- The Silent Generation fought thanklessly in the Korean conflict.
- They experienced little competition in sports, business, and the military as they moved up the ranks quickly into the void left behind by the huge GI Generation.
- The Silent Generation enjoyed very low unemployment.

- For its size, this generation had a healthy, yet relatively small crop of Generation X kids.
- They will cripple the assisted-living industry with their small numbers.
- Unlike the GI Generation, they do drive Japanese cars.

MARKETING TO THE SILENT GENERATION

You can successfully market to the Silent Generation with conventional media if you have a product that will enable them to maintain their independence for just a little while longer. They don't have misconceptions about staying young, but they don't want to be elderly, infirm, and reliant on their kids.

If you are in the assisted-living business, you can market to this group and their kids. However, you will never be able fill up your facility with the Silents because there simply are not enough of them to satisfy the exiting GI Generation footprint.

APPENDIX B
The Baby Boomers

The Baby Boom Generation apparently didn't like the world they lived in, the one they inherited from their parents, so they began to redefine things in the late sixties and early seventies. They produced their own music, art, movies, clothing, literature, cars, houses, and yes, marriages and families. They have their own vision—and they still plan to change the world.

Fast Facts about the Baby Boomers

- Born 1945 to 1964, they are 78 million strong, in a nice bell-shaped curve with its peak in 1957 to 1961. This peak defines markets—what will sell and what will not sell. The Boomers' peak is now cresting at fifty years old, an age when consumption traditionally begins to fall off precipitously. (However, if you have something to sell, don't count them out!)

- They fought against the "system"—learning to defy authority and not follow the rules set down for them by others.

- They helped accomplish great social change through the civil rights movement, the women's fight for equality, and anti-war protests.
- Many Boomers participated in the sexual revolution and the drug culture (at least smoked marijuana).
- They love to spend money on their children and grandchildren.
- Unfortunately, they have a hard time holding marriages together, evidenced by a 50 percent failure rate. Many Boomers routinely marry two and three times and raise multiple families.
- They often embrace slogans to define their lives: "Make love, not war." "Don't trust anyone over thirty." "Sixty is the new forty." "He who dies with the most toys wins."
- Baby Boomers are masters of conspicuous consumption with their Rolexes, SUVs, and starter castles.
- They are retiring at the rate of one every eight seconds.

MARKETING TO BABY BOOMERS

Baby Boomers remain the most powerful defined market in the world. True, the Boomers' spending is beginning to show chinks in the armor, but it will be a long time before the Boomers' consumption truly fades. Smart marketers will prosper by serving the front side of this generational wave generation for decades to come. Just remember the basics and use common sense.

If you want to do business with the Boomer you must:

- Make their life easy
- Save them some time
- Not try to rip them off

Marketing to the Boomers is not rocket science. You can reach them effectively and efficiently with conventional media.

- Radio, television, newspapers, billboards, magazines, and direct mail all work well when you want to reach the Boomer. (Just make sure your message is simple and your type is not too small.)
- The Internet is probably not an efficient way to the Boomer's heart. Remember, Boomers are immigrants in the cyberworld. Gen X and Gen Y are natives.

WHAT BOOMERS WILL BUY

The peak of the Baby Boomers is at the peak of their earning and consumption. Does that mean they are going to stop buying stuff? Yes, sort of. But they will buy anything that:

- *Will make them look and feel younger.* Remember, roughly 40 percent of Boomers are obese, with more getting fatter every day. This is a serious health issue that has the attention of heath insurance companies who are paying out huge dollars for weight-related maladies. As important as the health issue is, it is not the motivator that will cause Boomers to take drastic measures to change their body mass. The real motivator will be vanity. Boomers hate the way they look, but they are too lazy to exercise. Just on the horizon is a new service that will so please the insurance companies that they will pay the Boomers to go under the knife and have laparoscopic bariatric surgery. It's a win-win. Boomers get thin and healthier and insurance companies reduce their payout.

- *Is a natural remedy for what ails them.* Many Boomers truly believe that natural holistic medicines and treatments are best. While this approach may not be based in science, there is no denying its appeal and apparent success. Find a holistic remedy for aging and you will not be able to make it fast enough to satisfy the demand.

- *Will help the Boomers deal with their stuff.* Boomer's consumption will begin to wane as they crest fifty, but that does not mean they are willing to give up the stuff they already have. Why do you think there are so many self-storage places popping up? I really don't think this market is played out, because there is plenty of business to be had coming up with creative ways of dealing with

Boomers vast quantities of stuff. Call it "Stuff Care." You see, the Boomer really does believe that "He who dies with the most toys wins." The problem is the Boomer wants to have the stuff, but he does not want to care for it.

Boomers are deathly afraid of not having enough money to retire. This is probably because, in general, they don't have enough money to retire. So there is a huge market in helping Boomers overcome this dilemma.

- Financial services and retirement planning are going to be huge for aging Boomers.
- Retirement communities that are affordable will be overwhelmingly successful.

Boomers love to have fun, travel, and they are very social. They will take this attribute with them right into retirement.

- Remember, Boomers love to party, but instead of getting stoned and playing acid rock on their stereos like in the seventies, they watch the Super Bowl on their big screen TVs and drink beer and wine. If you can improve the party, you will have the Boomers' interest. Home entertainment centers with new features will continue to be very high on the Boomers' top-of-mind awareness. The Boomers will always buy what's new and hot.

- This may seem like a bit of a reach, but Boomers living in over-55 communities—especially those in proximity to a golf course—are demonstrating a penchant for customized golf carts with trick suspension and gas engines. I am forecasting that this will be a significant category as the Boomers age.

- Motor homes will be a major Boomer market in their own right, but the challenge will be to make them fuel efficient. Currently, these behemoths get less than ten miles to the gallon. That is not going to fly if we are paying $5 per gallon for fuel. In Europe, where gas is already through the roof, trailers are very popular, especially those that are very lightweight and pop up. A sure winner here in the States would be a real high-end lightweight pop-up that can be pulled by a car. The key here is high-end, full-featured, and secure. It can't be just for camping.

- The United States in general and the Boomers in particular are really falling out of love with the gas-guzzling SUV. May it rest in peace. (People who drive Hummers really make me wonder what they are thinking.) Boomers will be forced into smaller, more fuel-efficient cars. Keep in mind though that the Boomers must fit in the small cars comfortably and they must be easy to get in and out of.

- Don't forget alternative fuels and methods for heating and cooling the Boomer home. When gas spiked back in the seventies, a lot of Boomers turned to wood heat. Wood is not a solution for most of the aging Boomers. Wood is heavy and the process is difficult. That being said, many of the more hearty Boomers will buy chainsaws, wood splitters, and garden tractors in record numbers, especially in the Northeast. (It must be the toys thing.)

- The boating market has taken a real hit from the diminutive Generation X, but Boomers will cling to their traditions and love of fishing. Boats will be smaller and lighter and need to be fuel-efficient. Trailer able boats will remain popular, especially those that can be taken on and off by one person. Boomers are going to take their grandkids fishing. The big-boat market (30 to 60 feet) is history. Who can afford to run them?
- The bloom is off the rose for Boomer apparel. Most will simply dress for comfort as they put on pounds. Slip-on shoes will be the norm. Jewelry? They have enough and really don't have the need to impress anymore.
- Boomers love to eat, but just not as much. They will opt for home-cooked meals and takeout. Restaurants will suffer as Generation X can't pick up the slack.
- Cruises will remain strong. The concept works at multiple levels for the Boomer. Eat. Sit in a deck chair. Eat. Sit in a deck chair. Life is good.

- Funerals will change forever when the Boomers start to die on a large scale in about ten years. Rather than burials, there will probably be mostly cremations, with the ashes spread in creative ways. Boomers will resist rest homes with a vengeance.

APPENDIX C
Generation X

Following on the heels of the gigantic Baby Boomer Generation, with its let's-break-the-mold-and-start-a-whole-new-world attitude toward just about everything, Generation X is a strange story indeed. They are misunderstood, under-appreciated, and blamed for things out of their control—all as a result of their small numbers. Of course, Gen X didn't choose to be a tiny generation falling in between two monsters. It just happened that way. So have a little compassion for this bunch, even if you choose not to market to them.

Fast Facts about Generation X

- Gen Xers were born from 1965 to 1984, with a total of 69 million live births.
- They are advancing through time without the benefit of competition as they enter the infrastructure left behind by the Boomers.
- They are products of a small number of parents (Silent Generation), the impact of *Roe v. Wade*, improved

birth-control methods, and the prevailing concept of "zero population growth."

- Generation X will always live in the shadow of the larger Baby Boomer generation.
- They are constantly being told (falsely) that they are underachievers.
- Through no fault of their own, they are fated to always under-consume because they are too small a group to achieve Boomer consumption levels for almost everything.
- Because of its small size, Gen X closed many public schools, put Japanese motorcycle dealers in the U.S. out of business, and are vexations to Detroit's Big Three automobile companies.
- Generation X is too small a group to buy up the Boomers' starter castles, thus helping precipitate the U.S. housing crisis.
- In many cases, they adopted Boomers' culture, music, art, fashion, and recreation.
- Their lack of critical mass in the workforce and unwillingness to take bottom-of-the-food-chain entry-level jobs helped lead to massive Latino immigration, more than equal to Gen X's difference in size relative to the Boomers.

- Gen X will not be able to compensate for Boomers' health care costs in our current doomed shared-risk, private health care system.
- This small generation will not be able to sustain Social Security. (This is very serious.)
- They will not be able to pay enough taxes to run the local, state, and federal governments when it is their turn to carry the tax burden. (This is even more serious.)
- Generation X is creating management's perfect storm, because they do not have the critical mass needed to fill the management positions being exited by the Boomers as they retire.

MARKETING TO GENERATION X

Generation X can be successfully marketed to if you have a brand-new product or technology aimed specifically at their age demographic. All conventional products and services meet with disappointment because the Xers simply don't have the mass numbers to consume at the level of the Boomers who precede them.

You will need to market to this elusive group on the Internet because they shy away from most commercial television and radio and don't read newspapers or magazines. Good luck!

Generation X is not the doomsday generation. It is just a small generation right on the heels of a big generation. Once you understand the quantitative relationship of Generation X as compared to the Boomer Generation, you are light-years ahead of marketers who don't get it. Without an understanding of this basic concept of big and small, marketers are doomed to make frustrated attempts to try to make Generation X do something they can't.

APPENDIX D
Generation Y

We're still getting to know Generation Y as the top of the age group enters adulthood. They clearly have their own ideas and interests, things they are passionate about, and other things that don't interest them at all. They have grown up in an age of rampant technology; they are comfortable with and easily adaptable to all kinds of new gadgetry. Most important, we know that they dwarf the much smaller Generation X and are rapidly passing the Baby Boomers' population figures. While Generation Y is bigger than the Boomers in sheer numbers, they cannot outspend the Boomers until they have reached the Boomers' current income bracket.

Fast Facts about Generation Y

- They will be 100 million strong by 2010—the first twenty-five-year generation in over a hundred years.

- Gen Y contains a huge second-generation Latino contingent, especially on the young end.

- They are consuming at five times the rate of their Boomer parents in adjusted dollars.
- Gen Y will have large numbers of unemployed, and because of that, crime will spike.
- Because of their sheer numbers in the high-risk age demographic, sexually transmitted diseases (STDs) will spike (including AIDS), as will teen pregnancies.
- Generation Y will have a tremendous entrepreneurial spirit because of overwhelming unemployment.
- Gen Y will have a disproportionately high number of skilled technicians because of the huge demand and big salaries.
- They will own homes at a very young age because of high-paying tech jobs, successful businesses, and help from Boomer parents.
- Generation Y will embrace everything green. Green will be the legacy and calling card of Generation Y.

WHAT GEN Y WILL BUY

If Generation Y continues to consume at their current level, they are going to set retail sales records. I am forecasting that their appetite for stuff will only grow as they age. They consumed more expensive toys than any generation in our nation's history. Now they are moving on to the big stuff.

- They will continue to inhale anything electronic: Phones, computers, cameras, and iPods. Be aware that these devices are morphing into each other and may someday very soon be just one device.

- Clothes will be huge with this group as they begin to work their way toward finding a mate. Clothes are plumage and Generation Y will turn the apparel industry and the fashion world on its ear with their demands and consumption.

- Asian cars will be very strong with the Y Generation. They are already snapping up used Hondas, Toyotas, Subarus, Nissans, and Mitsubishis in a clear pattern that bodes well for these brands when Generation Y starts to buy new cars. Auto parts, accessories, and aftermarket tires and wheels will remain very healthy businesses overall because of the huge used-car market filled with Gen Y buyers.

- The Japanese motorcycle market should explode as Generation Y fills their narrow sixteen- to twenty-four-year-old male demographic with willing buyers. I say "should" because the Japanese manufacturers seem to be continuing to follow the shrinking Harley and Harley-clone Boomer market as it ages past its prime. The kids of Gen Y don't want low and slow. They want road rockets. Wake up, Japan!

MARKETING TO GENERATION Y

- If you want to do business with Generation Y, you better have a true green or humanitarian story tied to your product, service, or business culture. Don't try to "greenwash" or fake your green involvement because in their cyberworld information travels at light speed. This will play havoc with Wal-Mart and China and with products made cheaply with near slave labor.

- Marketing to Generation Y will be difficult because they use the Internet for much of their information and entertainment as opposed to TV, radio, newspapers, and magazines. This means that they will be difficult to brand because they are difficult to isolate with any media. While vast numbers of them do use the Internet, their use is fragmented. The Internet is the Wild West of media. The irony is that the generation with the potential of being the most consuming force in our nation's history will elude conventional marketing and branding. I rather suspect that the answer to this marketing conundrum will come from within Generation Y itself.

- Don't forget direct-mail advertising and snail mail. Generation Y loves to get snail mail and coupons. Go figure.

INDEX

ABOUT THE AUTHOR

Kenneth W. Gronbach is an internationally recognized expert in the field of demography and generational marketing. He is a marketing authority who regularly provides counsel to Fortune 500 companies, as well as large and small businesses across the United States.

Ken is an accomplished public speaker who engages audiences from many industries in public and private sectors throughout the country. He received his bachelor's degree in communications and public speaking from California State University at Long Beach. Ken consistently receives rave reviews from audiences and sponsoring organizations alike.

The author of many published articles, Ken has also been interviewed and written about extensively by the nation's press. He is a thought leader people turn to for his opinions about the generational impact on our social, political, and commercial landscape. His market research is ongoing and often quoted and copied.

An accomplished president and CEO, Ken has proved success in creating value, leading people, and planning for the future with uncanny accuracy. He led KGA Advertising for twenty-one years, growing it to a $40 million, forty-person marketing, advertising, and merchandising machine. KGA Advertising brought success to a diverse roster of retail and consumer clients and was the acknowledged catalyst for geometric growth in a large portion of its clients.

As leader of KGC Direct, Ken is internationally recognized for his uniquely accurate theories and his capability of predicting and forecasting marketing and societal phenomena.